by Larry G. Bowman

Captive Americans:

Prisoners During the American Revolution

OHIO UNIVERSITY PRESS: ATHENS, OHIO

Library of Congress Catalog Number 75-36984
ISBN 0-8214-0215-3 Cloth
ISBN 0-8214-0229-3 Paper
Printed in the United States of America
Designed by Harold M. Stevens

CONTENTS

Preface

The purpose of this book is to attempt to describe and evaluate the conditions which American military and civilian personnel endured as captives of the British military forces during the American Revolution. Several years ago, when I became interested in the prisoner of war issue in the Revolution, I began reading the diaries and memoirs of former American captives, and I soon concluded that the whole matter of American prisoners deserved a full-length study. Until recently historians have written little about the prisoners of war in the Revolution. The nineteenth and early twentieth centuries saw the appearance of numerous edited diaries or memoirs of captives, but no one produced a useful analysis of the writings of the American prisoners of war. The published diaries and memoirs were the chronicles of individual lives, and, while they were fascinating reading, the first hand accounts did little to educate their readers beyond recounting personal experiences. In addition, veterans of the British prisons were inclined to make extravagant and inaccurate statements which their editors frequently accepted at face value. As a result, the viewpoint most Americans accepted regarding the nature and intent of British policy toward American captives was the one presented by former prisoners of war. No one went beyond the perspective of the captives to explain why and how British prisoner of war policy evolved. So, in 1970, I began to research the prisoner of war issue with the hope of producing a balanced account of the saga of American captives from 1775 to 1782.

At the outset of this study, I entertained the notion of writing an account of the fate of the men detained by both warring camps of the

American Revolution. I soon abandoned that ambition however. My reasons for limiting my work to the American prisoners of war were twofold. A book dealing with British and American prisoner of war policies presented obvious problems in organization which bordered on the impossible to solve. And, secondly, a book detailing the treatment of both British and American captives promised a bulk of material too great for one volume. So, for reasons both cowardly and practical, I made the decision to examine only the American as prisoner of war.

When I began to write this volume, I made another decision regarding its contents which the reader will soon notice. I rarely quote directly from the first hand accounts of captives. The diaries and journals of prisoners do not lend themselves well to quotation. Entries in the accounts are usually fragmentary in detail, laconic in tone, and, when taken individually, surprisingly uninformative. What I have tried to achieve is a useful synthesis of the first hand accounts which detailed the hardships, frustrations, and observations of the captives without burdening the text with quotations.

The reader will also observe that I made another choice concerning the contents of this book. Few comparisons of American prisoner of war policy are drawn in relation to those of the British armed forces. I make no pretense whatsoever of examining American policy which governed the treatment accorded British captives. The moment I try to compare the policies of the belligerents, I begin to stray from my original purpose for this book. The reader will observe, on rare occasion, a fleeting comparison of the policies of the two nations, but the references are only safe generalizations and not detailed analysis.

Many people have helped me during the years of labor expended on this book. Librarians, archivists, and colleagues have assisted me in gathering information, listened to my ideas, and offered useful opinions. I thank them all. My wife and son, Sally and Curtis, have endured my many moods. They encouraged me, and they tolerated me when the need arose. I offer Sally and Curtis my loving thanks for their patience and understanding.

I also wish to express my gratitude to the Faculty Research Committee of North Texas State University. The committee provided me with financial assistance and released time from teaching duties to complete this project.

And finally, I wish to dedicate this book to the late Professor Raymond L. Welty. Professor Welty, who taught for thirty years at Fort Hays Kansas State College, led me down the path of history as an undergraduate, and I shall never forget him. He was the sort of gentleman, scholar, and teacher who had a profound impact on several generations of students. If this book has any merit, I dedicate it to him; if it is flawed, I reserve the criticism for myself.

Denton, Texas
July 4, 1975   L. G. B.

Captive Americans:
Prisoners During the American Revolution

chapter one

The Beginning

The treatment of Americans who were held prisoners of war by the British during the American Revolution provoked one of the most acrimonious quarrels which emerged from that conflict. Nearly every war produces a chronicle of suffering, neglect, and mistreatment of the men held captive, and the reactions of the belligerent nations involved are usually highly emotional, leaving a deep-seated bitterness when hostilities cease. The American Revolution was no exception. During the war, many men were taken captive in combat, and, as the revolution lasted for nearly seven years, there was plenty of time and reason for the prisoner of war question to become volatile.

Unfortunately for the men who suffer the fate of being made prisoners of war, the rules governing the treatment they are to receive from their captors have, until recent years, not been precisely defined or uniformly enforced. As a result, prisoners of war are frequently forced to endure great hardship, frustration, and despair while hoping for an early repatriation to their homes.

The prisoner of war is one of the most tragic figures in any struggle. He experiences a wide range of physical and emotional problems while awaiting an end to his captivity. The physical difficulties are the most obvious. He has little alternative but to try to survive on whatever food, clothing, quarters, medical care, and discipline his captors choose to provide. Emotional problems are not so obvious, but they have a devastating effect too. Fear, uncertainty, and boredom are only a few of the unsettling feelings a captive experiences. Few prisoners of war, in any war, have been able to describe adequately the emotional trauma they endured while being held captive, but there can be little doubt that their experiences were often terrifying and always unforgettable. Few people can understand what it means to live daily with fear. The prisoner never knows when his freedom will be restored, if he will be fed tomorrow, or if he will suddenly become the victim of some new shift in policy which will make his life even more difficult.

Consequently, the prisoner lives in a nightmare that is difficult to comprehend. Each day of his life holds the potential of the ultimate disaster he fears, and every detail of his captors' behavior is a matter he constantly analyzes, looking for reason to believe that this day will be one he can survive. One thing that all men who were ever prisoners of war seem to agree upon is that they never felt more vulnerable or helpless in any other time in their lives. The physical and emotional stress upon a captive is truly enormous. Americans who were taken captive in the Revolution contended with the same problems that, in one way or another, men in other conflicts have faced. The intensity of the suffering may vary somewhat in one war compared to another, but, basically, the hardships of the captives are the same.

It is apparent that, as the American Revolution got underway in April of 1775, no one had given much thought to the creation of a comprehensive plan to cope with the prisoner of war question which would inevitably arise. The Continental Congress was tangled in the problems of raising an army, dealing with all sorts of political and diplomatic issues, and building support among Americans for its position against Great Britain. The emerging state governments were equally preoccupied with similar issues. They, too, were concerned with enlisting troops, breaking down old loyalties to Great Britain, and consolidating their political position against the Crown.

The lack of consideration, on the part of the Continental Congress and on the part of the local governments, as to what policy was to be applied to protect American prisoners of war was standard. No one was worrying about this aspect of the coming war to any great degree. For those men enlisting in the Continental Army or in the state militias at that point, the inactivity was regrettable. Those men who were destined to become captives were to pay a high price for the lack of forethought and policy.

The British Army was not much better off in having developed any clear concept as to how Americans were to be handled as captives. Admittedly, the army had considerable experience with prisoners of war, but it was mostly with foreign troops and not with rebels. Usually the British Army followed certain standard procedures. Prisoners of war were allowed two-thirds the daily rations issued to a British soldier. Such matters as medical care, clothing, quarters, and the like were geared to meet the minimum requirements of captives. Ordinarily men taken prisoners of war in conflicts among the western powers in the eighteenth century did not long remain in enemy hands.[1] Great Britain was normally ready to make prisoner exchanges to recover badly needed manpower and to avoid the extra expense of caring for prisoners, but, in America, Great Britain was not dealing with a foreign enemy. Instead it was contending with an insurrection, and traditional patterns were not wholly applicable. For example, if the British Army entered into discussion with American authorities on such questions as standards of treatment of prisoners or the means of general exchange of captives, such negotiations might be construed as a tacit recognition of American independence, which was something the army had to try to avoid since this was a political matter beyond its scope of competence. As a result, the matters of prisons, treatment of prisoners, and their exchange were all complicated by special political considerations which the British Army was not fully prepared to meet.

When the Continental Congress became deeply concerned about the treatment of American captives and sought an agreement with the British to protect them, the British Army proved reluctant to enter into any formal agreements to establish standards of conduct toward prisoners. The reluctance was not caused by a lack of human compassion on the part of the British; it stemmed from the fact that the army had to consider the unique political circumstances which surrounded its activities in America.

Thus a combination of neglect and political complications was largely responsible for the absence of a truly coherent and effective policy governing the treatment of prisoners of war. Furthermore, neither the British nor the Americans realized that a lengthy struggle was to ensue, and, as a result, a well defined policy was absent in the beginning partially because few thought one necessary in a war which would not last long anyway.[2] Then as the war dragged on the issues became more complex, the possibility of a satisfactory solution to the fundamental problems attending the captives' plight became more remote. As is all too frequently the case, the prisoners became political pawns. Nobody really wanted this to happen, but it did. A good deal of the suffering endured by captives of both sides arose from the inability of the belligerents to achieve a political breakthrough and to arrive at a formal settlement to protect prisoners from the miserable conditions that became common in the Revolution. So the belligerents utilized any expedient they could devise to meet their responsibilities, and the prisoners were the victims of what could be best described as a haphazard code of conduct regarding the treatment of captured personnel.

Long before General William Howe launched his New York campaign in the summer of 1776, during which many Americans were captured, the problem of how to handle American prisoners began to materialize. In July of 1775, Captain Robert Mackenzie of the British Army recorded that twenty-seven rebels taken at Bunker Hill were being detained in Boston.[3] Later in the same year, Lord Dunmore, the last Royal Governor of Virginia, sent a group of prisoners to Boston from Virginia,[4] and, by early 1776, about three hundred Americans, who had been a part of the force which invaded Quebec in late 1775, were being held in the Seminary of Jesuits College in the City of Quebec.[5] The prisoner of war problem gradually began to demand attention. Then with Howe's first major campaign in 1776, which proved to be most successful, hundreds of Americans were taken captive, and at that point the problem became enormous. The issue could no longer be ignored, and the controversy began in earnest.

FOOTNOTES

[1] Olive Anderson, "The Treatment of Prisoners of War in Britain during the American War of Independence," *Bulletin of the Institute of Historical Research*, XXVIII (1955), 69. Cited hereafter as Anderson, "Treatment of Prisoners of War."

[2] Ira D. Gruber, *The Howe Brothers And The American Revolution* (New York, 1975), 198-99.

[3] List of Prisoners, Frederick Mackenzie Papers, William L. Clements Library, Ann Arbor, Michigan. Cited hereafter as Mackenzie Papers.

[4] George Washington to President of Congress, December 31, 1775, John C. Fitzpatrick, ed., *The Writings of George Washington*, 39 vols. (Washington, D.C., 1931-1944), IV, 197. Cited hereafter as Fitzpatrick, *Writings of Washington.*

[5] Major Return Meigs to George Washington, July 25, 1776, Jared Sparks, ed., *Correspondence of the American Revolution Being Letters of Eminent Men to George Washington*, 4 vols. (Boston, 1853), I, 265. Cited hereafter as Sparks, *Correspondence.*

chapter two

Prisoners of the British Army

Army personnel, Continental and state militia, were imprisoned in an astonishing variety of places and types of prisons during the Revolution. When they were first taken in combat, American prisoners of war were temporarily detained in the general vicinity where they were captured so they could be used in exchanges for British troops who had fallen into American hands in the recent action or campaign. How long an American remained a prisoner in the locality where he was captured depended upon many factors. The British Army always needed manpower, and it was normally quick to make local, informal exchanges of prisoners without any long range agreement or treaty to govern future exchanges. So, if a prisoner was lucky, he might be held only a short time before he was exchanged and allowed to return to American lines. If a local exchange could not be effected, or if there were American prisoners remaining after an exchange was completed, then the usual practice was to move them to New York City where they would be offered for exchange at a later date.

Prisoners were also moved to other areas if the British Army considered its grip on a theater of combat uncertain. In a case such as this, New York City nearly always was the ultimate destination of prisoners of war from a disputed battlefield. When possible, the British Army tried to keep prisoners near the site of their capture, as they hoped this would encourage rapid trading of captives. Local exchanges were encouraged by the British Army for several reasons. First, and most obviously, it was an easy means to recover lost and valuable manpower. Secondly, local exchanges reduced the demands for food, clothing, and fuel by regional commanders who had the responsibility to care for their prisoners. The army had enough problems caring for its own people, Loyalists, and Indian allies. Burdens which the British Army could shed easily were happily discarded. And finally, of course, rapid local exchanges had their propaganda value, which British authorities reasoned would help undermine support among the colonials for the Revolution. A defeated soldier who was returned to his comrades served the dual purpose of demonstrating the invincibility and the humanity of the British Army. The British were not unmindful of such uses of exchanges, but, on the other hand, the army did not exploit this feature as much as it probably should have.

Basically, the British attitude toward prisoners was not a vindictive one. When the opportunities for local exchanges were exhausted, the remainder of prisoners of war were moved elsewhere for repatriation, and, as mentioned before, New York City was the destination for these men the British Army sought to exchange after local arrangements had been exhausted. Before discussing New York City as the main center of detention and exchange of American Army personnel, several other locations must first be mentioned.

The prisons in which Americans were confined, aside from the elaborate system in the New York City area, shared several characteristics. Prison compounds outside New York were usually small and temporary. If a regional prison became overcrowded the overflow was transferred to another area — usually to New York. Regional prisons were hastily organized, and they were, as a rule, inadequate for the needs of both the captor and the captive. In the thirteen colonies, regional prisons never functioned very long because the British never held on to any particular section of the country, except for New York City, for more than two years or so. Because of the changing patterns of the war, the locations of the prisons shifted too. As the emphasis of the war shifted from one section of the colonies to another, it was only natural that the permanent garrison of New York City played the major role in the prisoner of war question.

As was mentioned in chapter one, the first American prisoners of war were confined in Boston, Massachusetts. Actually, Boston's role as the site of a British prison was a small and brief one. Not more than a few dozen men were held or exchanged there before the British evacuated the town in 1776. Among the earliest sites of significant prisoner of war activity were Quebec and Halifax, Nova Scotia. In September, 1775, thirty-four militiamen were incarcerated in the public jail in Quebec. These soldiers had been captured in New York and brought to Quebec, and they were finally sent to Boston and exchanged in early 1776.[1]

Reports of captives being held in Halifax begin in early 1776 and continue until the end of the war.[2] Although the presence of Americans as captives in Canada was common throughout the war, the numbers of them held there were never great. Most of the captives in Quebec and Halifax were remnants of the 1775-76 invasion of Canada led by Benedict Arnold and Richard Montgomery, or captives made by Indians on raids into New York, Pennsylvania, and New England, or prisoners taken during General John Burgoyne's invasion of the Hudson River valley in 1777.

All sorts of buildings were used to house the captives held in Canada. The most commonly employed were the public jails, warehouses, abandoned structures, and any other type of building which could be put into temporary service. In the city of Quebec, the public jail and the facilities at Jesuits' College were used to hold prisoners.[3] The main center for the detention of prisoners in Halifax was a large one story building on Hollis Street called the Old Jail.[4]

Anything which could easily be converted into a prison compound, with only little regard for the comforts such an arrangement provided the inmates, was employed when the available jails were filled with captives. The crucial factors considered by the army were that such prisons could be opened quickly, operated cheaply, and then abandoned with little difficulty when the need for them was ended. Consequently, a pattern began to emerge early in the war. Prisoners of war were viewed as an inconvenience, and the British Army decided to provide only the minimum of support to its captives. The decision was not one arrived at in a dramatic fashion, it simply evolved over several months of practice.

At the outset of the war, the British Army operated on the premise that the struggle would not last very long and that more permanent, comfortable accommodations were unnecessary. The result was, of course, a rather haphazard prison system predicated on temporary answers to what became a lengthy and complicated issue. The British Army was governed by two imperatives. One was to provide adequate (though often barely so) facilities, and the second was to minimize expenses by using whatever expedients it could devise in housing, feeding, and clothing the prisoners under its care. The sufferings of the American captives resulted more from this policy than from malice.

For a few months, from the end of 1777 into the summer of 1778, the British Army occupied Philadelphia and, of course, prisoners of war were located there too. Since the British presence in Philadelphia was of short duration the situation there regarding prisoners was a fluid one. Regular prison compounds were not established. Instead, the British confined American enlisted men in the public jails and billeted the officers in the state capitol.[5] For a brief period, Philadelphia played a minor role as a center of detention and exchange of small numbers of prisoners, but this ended abruptly when the British evacuated Philadelphia in June of 1778.

Elsewhere in North America other prisons were established by the British Army. As early as 1778, a few Americans were kept captive at St. Augustine, Florida.[6] Then, after the British seized Charleston, South Carolina, in 1780, large numbers of South Carolina militia were incarcerated at St. Augustine.[7] Other captured personnel taken during the collapse of the defense of Charleston were managed locally. Most of the militia defenders of Charleston, except those sent to St. Augustine, were paroled and allowed to return to their homes to await official exchange.[8] The paroles stipulated that the militiamen agreed not to bear arms against Great Britain until they were exchanged. The Continental forces captured in Charleston were less fortunate. They were placed in prisons in and around the city.

The fall of Charleston was the worst defeat the United States suffered in the war. More than five thousand American troops were taken captive when General Benjamin Lincoln surrendered the city to the British. The British authorities were almost overwhelmed with captives, so, in addition to paroling most of the militia and sending the remainder to St. Augustine, they had to detain many prisoners in the Charleston area.

As usual, the British looked for the same kinds of facilities which they had used as prisons elsewhere. The public jails were soon filled with the captives, so a special prison camp was opened at Haddrell's Point near Charleston where the Continental troops were confined. A few captured American soldiers and many American naval prisoners were placed aboard prison ships anchored in Charleston harbor.[9] The Charleston area was dotted with all descriptions of prisons to handle the mass of captives taken when the city capitulated to the British.

A much smaller prison system than the one in Charleston was created in Savannah, Georgia, after that city was taken by the British in 1778.[10] The procedure in Savannah was to follow the familiar pattern and employ public jails, public buildings, and empty structures to house the small number of men held captive there. Over and over again, the British Army used about the same solutions in each area and requisitioned the same types of quarters for its captives.

A few very unfortunate American soldiers were held in prisons outside North America. In January of 1777, sixteen Americans were sent from Quebec to Senegal in Africa. Benjamin Franklin issued several futile protests, while serving at his diplomatic post in Paris, over this action.[11] Several Americans were sent from the colonies to Antigua in the West Indies,[12] and a goodly number of soldiers, perhaps four hundred, were transferred to England from South Carolina.[13] The number of army personnel sent from North America to Europe, to the West Indies, to Africa, or elsewhere outside of the thirteen colonies was small, but the practice, which was largely confined to the early and uncertain years of the war, was deeply resented and bitterly attacked by American military and political figures.

New York City was the site of several big prisons which were established in 1776-77 and operated for the duration of the war. By virtue of the facts that New York City was the main garrison of the British Army in America and that the New York campaign of 1776 yielded a host of American captives, the army was obliged to create a large prison system in the city. Additionally, the practice of sending surplus prisoners to New York from outlying military districts tended to keep the New York prisons heavily populated. As a result, New York City and Long Island became the cornerstones of the whole prison complex the British developed during the Revolution.

Beginning in the autumn of 1776, several prisons were opened in New York, and all of them were destined to become notorious before the war ended. One of the first was the Provost, which was located in the Old Jail; the Old Jail later was known as the Hall of Records after the war.[14]

The Provost was a three story building in which the first floor served as quarters for the Provost Marshal and the guard. The second and third floors were converted into cells to accommodate prisoners. On the second floor in the northeast corner of the building, a chamber, called Congress Hall, was used to detain high ranking American captives.[15] Nearly all officers above the rank of colonel were placed under tight restriction, usually in the Provost. Among the famous men who visited Congress Hall as a prisoner was Ethan Allen.[16]

Basically, however, the Provost was a place where all manner of persons were detained. The reports of the Provost Marshall list inmates of varying descriptions. Unruly American prisoners who tried to escape or who were difficult to control were placed in the Provost to learn some discipline. Civilians suspected of espionage, local criminals, and derelicts of all types were, from time to time, to be found there too.[17] The number of inmates usually detained in the Provost was few. From the reports filed by the Provost Marshal to Sir Henry Clinton's headquarters, there were as few as four and as many as sixty-one men detained there at one time or another.[18] Consequently, the Provost was not a common prison, and it was instead reserved for special functions. The Provost was not crowded and it was relatively clean and spacious, but it had an unsavory history. William Cunningham, the Provost Marshal, had a reputation for being harsh with the prisoners, and among Americans he was well known and feared.[19] The Provost remained in operation until the final day of British occupation of

New York City, which helped to place it high among the most despised of British prisons.[20]

On December 3, 1776, General William Howe, the Commander in Chief of British forces in America, recorded that his command held no less than 4,430 American troops as prisoners of war resulting from the New York and New Jersey campaigns of that year.[21] The difficulties of caring for so many captives were especially burdensome with the coming of winter. There were only two jails in New York City in the autumn of 1776 suitable to detain prisoners. One was the Old Jail, which was selected to serve as the Provost, and the other was New Bridewell, which was used to imprison privates from the Continental and militia units.[22] A partial answer to the pressing problem of too many captives and too few prisons was to release enlisted men, especially from the militia, who would probably return to their homes and pose no immediate threat to Howe's army. According to Ambrose Serle, somewhere in the neighborhood of two thousand enlisted men were released without exchange for British captives and allowed to return to their homes to spread the message of Howe's humanity and the futility of further resistance to the British Army.[23] After the release of the two thousand men, Howe still had more than two thousand men in his custody, and, at that point, the search for additional facilities to detain the men began in the last part of 1776.

Three sugar houses along the waterfront area of New York City which were used to store rum, sugar, and molasses were converted into prisons to help to meet the demands placed on the British Army to house its captives.[24] Van Courtland's sugar house, located on the northeast corner of Trinity Churchyard, and Rhinelander's sugar house, on the corner of William and Duane Streets, were commandeered by the army and refitted to serve as prisons.[25] The two warehouses were instrumental in helping to provide badly needed space for captives, but it was the Liberty Street sugar house which was the largest and the most infamous of the three sugar house prisons.[26] The Liberty Street building was a somber five story structure which had a small fenced yard where the prisoners were allowed to exercise. Its windows were covered with boards, and little interior renovation was made. The Liberty Street prison, while it was fairly spacious, lacked adequate sanitary facilities, and it was spartan in its appearance and furnishings. Van Courtland's and Rhinelander's sugar house-prisons were small, but they were essentially imitations of the Liberty Street prison. Van Courtland's and Rhinelander's sugar houses were used in 1776 and 1777, and then closed down after the number of prisoners began to dwindle due to several prisoner of war exchanges and a slowdown in military activities. Even when these two sugar houses were in service, the term "sugar house" was used to designate the Liberty Street prison. After Van Court-land's and Rhinelander's prisons were closed in 1777, the confusion about the sugar house-prisons among the Patroits was finally ended. The Liberty Street sugar house was used to confine enlisted men throughout most of the war, and it became well known as a result.[27]

The sugar houses were not well maintained. They tended to be dirty, too hot in the summer, and too cold in the winter. In winter, especially, the prisoners suffered in the sugar houses. Captives rarely had enough fuel for heating the drafty prisons. One of the inmates of the Liberty Street prison later wrote that while he was held there the prisoners were allowed fuel every third day.[28] The sugar houses were a partial, although unsatis-factory, answer to an urgent problem. Eventually, as Van Courtland's and Rhinelander's houses were phased out of service, the army began to try to improve conditions in the Liberty Street prison, but the success in doing so was minimal.

The sugar houses were not a total answer to the desperate need for quarters for the prisoners held in New York City in the winter of 1776-77. Many more men were in custody than the army was prepared to receive, and other expedients had to be employed to satisfy the demands for billets for the captured Americans. A number of churches were pressed into ser-vice as prisons. From the beginning, the churches were viewed as tempora-ry quarters, and they were eventually phased out as prisons by the latter part of 1777, or converted into hospitals to care for prisoners of war. Brick Church, North Dutch Church, Middle Dutch Church, Quaker Meeting House, Presbyterian Church, Scot Church, and French Church were all employed as prisons for the influx of captives in 1776-77.[29]

The churches were poorly equipped to meet the needs of the men con-fined in them, and the inmates of the churches experienced about the same hardships as those in the other prisons. The captives in the churches were crowded, cold, and hungry. They lacked proper clothing, bedding, and sufficient amounts of fuel to warm themselves or to cook their meager rations. Gradually the churches were to be removed from service as prisons in 1777, but Brick Church, Presbyterian Church, Scot Church, and Friend's Meeting House were then converted to duty as hospitals, and they were utilized as such until the early 1780's.[30] According to Elias Boudinot, who visited the hospitals in February of 1778, they were clean, and the sick were well cared for in the church-hospitals. In fact, Boudinot was pleasantly surprised over the conditions in the hospitals, and he com-mended them with reserved praise.[31]

In addition to the already mentioned locations, King's College and City Hall also saw service as prisons and hospitals.[32] At least thirteen separate prisons were established in New York City in 1776-77. Most of these thirteen hastily created prisons functioned for only a short time. The Liberty Street prison, the Provost, and New Bridewell continued to operate until the end of the war as the primary detention centers for American captives.

Not all captured American personnel were forced to survive in the gloomy prisons. Captured American officers were treated in a little different fashion from the rank and file of the American forces. During the winter of 1776-77, when so many prisoners were crowding New York City, the British Army began the practice of separating the American officers from their men and placing them under confinement outside the prisons where the men were detained. Segregating the officers from the men served several purposes. First, the prisons were overcrowded, and by locating the officers elsewhere a little relief was afforded the inmates of the overtaxed facilities. Secondly, a more important reason for removing the officers from contact with men was to replace the officers' authority with British discipline, which the British hoped would render the American prisoners of war more docile and manageable. And finally, of course, the British Army had a practical reason for according American officers better treatment and conditions. A number of British officers were in American hands, and setting a generous example might ensure that his Majesty's officers would receive better consideration while awaiting exchange.

Providing special quarters for captured American officers turned out to be a fairly simple matter for the army to solve. One of two means was applied to most of the situations. As the winter of 1776 drew near, the prisons, churches, hospitals, and prison ships were heavily burdened with American personnel,[33] so the British Army inaugurated the practice of permitting carefully chosen residents of New York City to take in captured officers as boarders.[34] The officers were paroled and allowed the freedom of the city. Paroled Americans were pledged, upon their honor as gentlemen, not to try to escape or to engage in sabotage or espionage. Furthermore, American officers living in private dwellings on parole were expected to pay for their room and board from whatever private funds they possessed or by using credit their landlords might agree to extend them.[35]

How many American officers were permitted this amount of freedom is virtually impossible to determine. The narratives of John Adlum and Jabez Fitch, two Americans who were prisoners of war and lived on parole in the city, abound with references to officers living in all sections of town.[36] Then in early 1777, the second means of farming out American officers in private dwellings began. The city of New York was saturated with prisoners, Loyalists, military and naval personnel, and refugees, which reduced the opportunities of placing more American officers in private homes. To help to alleviate the congestion and to provide more areas for the officers to find suitable quarters, commissioned officers were allowed to seek quarters in private homes among the villagers on the southwestern end of Long Island. Such villages as Flatbush, Flatlands, New Eutrecht, Gravesend, Bedford, and New Lots were soon heavily populated with American officers who were paroled and living in private homes.[37] The paroles specified the area through which the officers could roam, but to go beyond the stipulated area required special permission from General Howe's staff. Parole violators were sent to the Provost which was usually enough to intimidate most men.[38] The practice of quartering officers in New York City and on Long Island continued, on a lessening scale, until the struggle was finished.[39]

The quarrel which developed between the British and American authorities over the treatment that the American military personnel received was not long in coming. On August 11, 1775, General George Washington issued his first formal protest. In a letter to Lieutenant General Thomas Gage, the British Commander in Chief headquartered in Boston, Washington complained about the conditions American prisoners of war in Boston were forced to endure. Washington began, at this point, a long series of complaints which became monotonously familiar before the war was concluded. He specified several matters which disturbed him regarding the treatment of captives. Washington expressed his anger that American prisoners of war were lodged in the public jail with felons, as he put it, and that the clothing, food, and other necessaries of life issued to the prisoners were inadequate.[40]

Washington was worried about the men being held in Boston, but he had another motive behind his letter. Most of all he wanted to establish an understanding with General Gage that captured Americans were in fact prisoners of war, and, as such, were entitled to certain conduct on the part of their captors. If the captives were to be treated as rebels, then they were vulnerable to any form of reprisal the British might wish to inflict, an eventuality the American Commander in Chief wished to forestall if at all possible. In these early and uncertain months, no one knew exactly how the captured men should be handled, and General Washington was trying to establish the viewpoint that the men held in Boston were prisoners of war and not rebels. The welfare of the men held in Boston was at stake, true enough, but so was the safety of the men who would be captured in later engagements. General Washington was not unmindful of the important precedents about to be established in 1775.

Gage answered with a firm but polite letter in which he neatly sidestepped the main thrust of Washington's letter. He wrote that it was true that American prisoners were lodged in public jails, but that they were treated with kindness. Furthermore, Gage argued that their rations were sufficient, and that Washington's fears for the safety of his men were unfounded.[41] Gage went on to point out in his response to Washington's letter that the use of the jail was his only means of imprisoning the men, and that Washington should not be alarmed about the use of a public jail to detain the captives. The routine reassurance of the well-being of the captives, and the fact that Gage refused to commit himself on the issue of whether the Americans were to be considered as prisoners of war, was of little comfort to General Washington. So, early in the conflict, the battle over the definition of the status of the American soldiers seized while under arms against Great Britain was joined. After General Gage served as Commander in Chief, his successors, Generals William Howe, Henry Clinton, and Guy Carleton, also maintained a copious and sometimes sharp correspondence with Washington on the prisoner of war question. They, too, proved equally reluctant to discuss the legal status of the Americans as prisoners of war.

For the men who were captured, certain events and reactions were fairly common among them the first few days they were prisoners. At first, the soldiers had to cope with the shock and dismay which settled upon them when they realized they were, or were about to become, captives. A feeling of panic and then of despair was the usual cycle of emotion the prisoners experienced. During the initial day or so after their capture the prisoners were penned in old barns, abandoned houses, or other available structures on or near the battlefield where they had been seized. Because of the confused conditions which prevailed in a combat area, the prisoners usually experienced their first tribulations almost immediately. Accompanying the emotional turmoil which inevitably plagued new prisoners, they also normally lacked proper bedding and food, and their makeshift prisons were always crowded and often unsanitary. The prisoners were, considering the difficulties the British Army faced in trying to provide for them under combat conditions, usually treated fairly well. A good many of the American captives, however, were stripped of such possessions as money, watches, rings, and other valuables in the first day or so of their captivity.[42] They were subjected to verbal taunts and, occasionally, to some physical abuse although the latter was not common.[43]

Then when the prisoners were transferred to a more permanent prison they often endured a good deal of jeering and taunting from the unsympathetic local citizenry in the area where they were to be detained.[44] The first few days were especially confusing as the men learned to accept their new status and acquainted themselves with the routine and humiliation of being prisoners of war.

Once the captives were moved from the battle zone into prisons, they came under the jurisdiction of a special department of the British Army known as the Commissary of Prisoners headed by the Commissary General for Prisoners. While the first few days of captivity were traumatic ones for the captives, they were not, as a rule, treated too badly by their captors. Having their valuables taken, suffering verbal assaults, and so forth were extremely difficult to accept, but the American prisoners were rarely the victims of some of the really barbarous atrocities sometimes committed upon prisoners of war. Murder, torture, and the other vicious deeds often perpetrated upon helpless captives seldom occurred when the Americans fell into British hands.

The British Army was not only slow to establish a general policy regarding American prisoners, it was also slow in creating a permanent department to exercise authority over its captives. Until the latter part of 1776 the prisoners were cared for in a haphazard fashion, but after the New York campaign the vast numbers of captives demanded more time and attention. So in early 1777 Joshua Loring was appointed to the post of Commissary General for Prisoners to supervise the prisons in New York and to watch over the well-being of all captives of the British Army in America.[45] As Commissary for Prisoners, Loring reported directly to the Commander in Chief who, at that point, was General William Howe. Final authority on all matters concerning the prisoners resided with the Commander in Chief, but the day-to-day administration of the prisons and the prisoners' lives was the duty of Loring.[46]

Joshua Loring was an American Loyalist who was born in Hingham, Massachusetts, in 1744. He and his wife left Boston with the British Army when it repaired to Halifax, Nova Scotia, in 1776.[47] Loring and his wife attracted Howe's attention and eventually his friendship. Their friendship rewarded Loring in the form of his commission. The relationship of Loring, Mrs. Loring, and General Howe was, and still is, much discussed. Perhaps the bluntest statement is in Thomas Jones' *History of New York During the Revolutionary War* in which he accused Loring of all manner of crimes. Jones wrote that while Loring ". . . fingered the cash, the General enjoyed Madam."[48] Indeed, Joshua Loring was an unusual man, but, nevertheless, he was the Commissary General for Prisoners and the fate of thousands of men rested with his office.

Under Loring's direction, with General Howe's knowledge and consent, the basic policies for the care and provisioning of the American prisoners were devised. When the prisoners of war were first captured they had to be content with whatever meager rations the British Army could supply them in the field. In the battlefield environment the difficulties of properly caring for the men were not unanticipated, and they were tolerated by the combatants. When, however, the captives were placed in prisons and controlled by a regular routine the situation was different. The British Army had to assume a deeper responsibility for their welfare, and it had to establish a standard policy for provisioning the prisoners.

On the question of the food rations issued to the American prisoners by the British, the American authorities were never totally satisfied with the amount and quality. As early as January 17, 1777, the Continental Congress expressed its alarm over the manner in which the American captives, located mostly in New York City at this juncture, were being provisioned.[49] Washington had already written to Howe protesting the conditions his men faced, and the action by Congress was designed to lend support to the Commander in Chief's campaign to improve the lot of the Americans in British prisons.[50] A sizeable correspondence between Washington and Howe developed over the question of food for the captives. The British position throughout the war, with some alterations due to local emergencies or difficulties, was to put the captives on two-thirds the normal rations issued to the British soldier on duty.[51] Regardless of whether an American was a prisoner in New York in 1777, or in Philadelphia in 1778, or in Charleston in 1780, or at any other place at any other time under the jurisdiction of the British Army, he normally received the standard two-thirds ration.

In 1778, in response to another of Washington's letters demanding improved rations for his men in captivity, General Howe carefully outlined the British Army's program for provisioning its captives.[52] According to Howe, the rations allotted to an American prisoner amounted to four pounds ten and two-thirds ounces of bread, and three pounds eight ounces of meat per week. Howe went on to point out that if supplies permitted the basic meat and bread rations were varied, and the prisoner received four pounds ten and two-thirds ounces of bread, two pounds ten and two-thirds ounces of meat, two pints of peas, four ounces of butter, and five and one-third ounces of oatmeal a week.[53] Naturally, General Howe indicated his belief that the amount of food issued to the captives was quite sufficient for men not on active duty. Howe's argument seems plausible if the first premise is accepted that the full ration issued to the British soldier on duty was sufficient, which it probably was not.[54] British troops were able to supplement their rations, but the prisoners frequently lacked that opportunity, so they had to endure on what was an inadequate diet.[55] While the British Army appeared convinced that the two-thirds ration was enough food for the captives, it did allow them to buy extra food from vendors outside the prisons or to receive gifts of food from sources they might legally develop.[56]

It must be emphasized, however, that while the food issued the American prisoners was probably inadequate in amount, to say nothing of its quality or nutritional value, the shortage was not the result of a willful policy of persecution. Instead, it was an unfortunate result arising from the neglect and almost traditional mistreatment of the British soldier, who also was expected to survive on a rather stingy policy. The American citizen-soldier who had never before paid much attention to the plight of British soldiers learned, as a prisoner of war, how much they had to endure in peace and war. Few Americans who were prisoners of war were likely to forget the two-thirds ration they received, and the more perceptive among them must have learned to appreciate the British soldier's sacrifice which serving in his Majesty's army required.

American officers fared a little better than the enlisted men while in captivity. The officers who were placed in the prisons drew the two-thirds food ration as did everyone, but they were usually moved out of the prisons, placed on parole, and allowed to make arrangements for food and lodgings among the local inhabitants authorized by the British Army to take in American officers as roomers and boarders. As a result, the officers suffered less from the lack of sufficient food than did the enlisted men.[57] As a rule, the officers were charged two dollars a week for their room and board.[58] Many of the officers, in the early years, paid the two dollars from whatever personal funds they possessed or lived on credit with the promise to pay when they received funds. Eventually, the Continental Congress authorized money to be sent to the officers so they could pay their bills regularly.[59] The landlords with whom the officers lived provided a room, bedding, and three meals a day. The rooms were often crowded with two or more men, and the food was adequate although the officers complained of monotonous meals. Nevertheless, the officers lived under better circumstances than their men.

Inadequate clothing was nearly as worrisome to the prisoners as the insufficient food allotments. When men were first seized on the battlefield it was common for much of their clothing to be taken from them.[60] Items such as boots, shoes, and coats were regularly stolen, and the prisoners faced the nearly insurmountable problem of trying to survive without them. Reports of American prisoners of war suffering from the want of decent clothing began in 1776 and continued for the balance of the war.[61] The British were much more negligent about providing clothing and bedding for captives than they were about food rations. Apparently, there was no set policy as to when captives were to receive clothing and bedding; for that matter, there was no guideline regulating what amounts of bedding and clothing the captives were to receive when issues were made.

Basically, the British program revolved around the hope that the prisoners would be quickly exchanged and that the expenses of food, clothing, and bedding could be avoided or, at least, severely reduced. When, however, the exchange of captives was delayed, as it often was, by all sorts of technicalities, and the prisoners languished in prison for months, their lack of new garments became critical. Under prison routine a suit of clothes soon wore out with the constant, hard use. A prisoner was soon in need of new apparel, and as a change in season approached his needs changed. A soldier captured on Long Island in August of 1776 was hardly prepared to endure a winter in one of the sugar houses unless he obtained heavier clothing. Many men, tragically, did not get the necessary clothing, and their chances of surviving the winter months were reduced because of it.

Periodically the British did, of course, issue some clothing and bedding to the prisoners, but these distributions were sporadic and partial in effect.[62] More often than not, when a large issue of clothing was made to the prisoners by Loring's department, it came at the beginning of winter. Unfortunately, there was never enough for all the prisoners, so some were left with their needs unattended. Issuing clothing at the start of winter had its obvious humane purpose, but the propaganda value of such timing was deemed of nearly equal importance by the British.

To obtain extra garments, the men had to turn to auxilliary sources to assist them. In the early months of the war, their best hope was to receive gifts of clothing from concerned persons outside the prisons. Officers on parole, local Patriots, clergymen, and humanitarians of all sorts collected clothing and delivered it to the prisons to help the men.[63] In addition to local donations of clothing, inmates who had been tailors in civilian life were permitted to make garments for their fellow prisoners from materials donated for that purpose. Among the prisoners there was a brisk market for the apparel of deceased inmates and for the garments of men about to be exchanged. Men about to leave a prison in an exchange usually left as much of their clothing with the men remaining behind as they could afford to leave plus all their bedding and other items they could spare.[64] All of these means did not come anywhere near supplying the prisoners' requirements. Finally, the Continental Congress assumed the responsibility of attempting to keep the prisoners furnished with decent clothing.[65] In spite of all the efforts of Congress and those of private donors, the clothing and bedding shortage among the captives continued during the entire conflict.

Meidcal care for the American prisoners was also insufficient. Men who were wounded at the time they were captured usually received medical attention equal to that the British soldier enjoyed.[66] Captured Americans were treated in whatever field hospitals the British had established and then transferred to army or prison hospitals as the local circumstances dictated. For all practical purposes, the American had better medical care on the battlefield if he was a prisoner than if he was still with his own unit.[67] The British Army surgeons were, to be fair, faced with great odds in their struggle to save men, but they performed their tasks with dedication and a moderate degree of success. Many Americans profited from their services. Eighteenth century military medicine was not very complete by modern standards, obviously, but the British Army had a good record in looking to its wounded and also in giving wounded captives all the medical care available.

Among healthy or injured captives confined in the prisons the British medical program was more vulnerable to criticism. Actually there was no regular medical program for the prison inmates. American surgeons who were prisoners themselves were allowed to visit the men and do what they could for them, but their numbers were few and their resources were limited.[68] The American surgeons actually accomplished little. Essentially, the British policy was to disregard the medical needs of the captives once they entered the prisons. Such matters as inoculation, regular inspection of prisoners, enforcement of sanitary measures, isolation of the desperately ill, and other types of preventive medicine were almost unknown. The result was an alarming death rate in the British Army prisons especially during the winter months. Ordinarily, a prisoner's medical needs were ignored until he became gravely ill. Then he might be moved to a hospital, if there was room for him there, and put under medical care. The hospitals were clean and neat, but there were too few of them, and those that did exist were too small in the patient load they could accommodate.[69] For most of the stricken captives the hospital was a place to die and not a place to recover. An energetic program of inspection and care of prisoners daily environment plus regular visits from physicians coupled with enough nutritious food and appropriate clothing would probably have reduced the death rate among the prisoners.[70]

The question of the quality of the medical attention provided to American prisoners was never satisfactorily answered so far as the American authorities were concerned.[71] It has to be noted, however, that harsh judgment of the British failure to supply adequate medical care to the prisoners must be tempered by the realization that the sufferings of the prisoners arose from neglect rather than from premeditated cruelty. Neglect of the medical requirements of prisoners, not to mention the needs of their own personnel, was common in both armies. The treatment of prisoners of war certainly reflected some of the assumptions of the eighteenth century mind regarding life and death.

One of the smaller issues, at least on a numerical scale, was the British policy of imprisoning civilians on all types of charges. The American authorities were especially sensitive on this point, as the British obviously had the advantage in such a matter. If the British Army decided to begin wholesale arrests of American civilians, for whatever reasons it might declare, there were no real means of retaliation open to the Continental Congress or to the states. Many civilians were incarcerated by the British forces during the war, and another bitter, intense controversy swirled about the non-combatant captives.

Every American agency of government from the Continental Congress down to the state governments regularly protested the British practice of seizing civilians. All the protests failed to bring an end to the civilian arrests by the British. The state governments did try to help the citizens after they were imprisoned by the British, but nothing could be done about the arrests in advance. The British forces could arrest persons anywhere at any time, and nothing could be done to protect the people from arbitrary imprisonment. About all that could be done was to protest the arrests and demand the release of the individuals that the British had, in the view of Congress and the states, seized illegally.

The British retorted, naturally, that the arrests were justified by the fact that the apprehended persons had not remained circumspect in their conduct. For the British, once they occupied an enemy area, one of the most difficult matters a conquering army has to face arose. The occupying force must live in a location where an open, active animosity, even if it is only a minority attitude, must be anticipated. Any army must develop a security system for its personnel in the area it has just invaded. In addition to protecting its men, the invading army must also try to prevent an outbreak of lawlessness, which often accompanies an invasion, to protect the local inhabitants from being victimized as well. The first step, therefore, is for the occupying force to gain control of such local institutions as civil government, police, and other agencies to provide for the continuation of necessary public services. This requires that one of three conditions prevail among the local officials: local leaders must prove cooperative; they must be neutralized; or, if the worst comes, they must be imprisoned to allow the occupying force time to gain firm control over the area it has just conquered. The simplest way to secure local control is to isolate the natural leaders of a community from the populace, for a short time at least, while the transition from civil to military government is being accomplished. An occupying force must quickly suppress all forms of resistance to provide safety for itself and to win the support of its sympathizers. In almost every community in America during the Revolution there was a substantial number of people who were indifferent to the political and military affairs which surrounded them and who desired only stability.[72] So the British Army resorted to firm measures to insure its control over captured enemy territory. Winning the battle to gain control over an area was only one-half the struggle the British Army had to wage. It also had to contend with the very delicate task of imposing its will upon the inhabitants once the military issue was decided. American Patriots, of course, were adamant in their allegations that the British were much too stern, and that what the army chose to view as efforts to establish law and order were, in reality, a means of intimidating the public. A fundamental difference of opinion concerning the motivation of the British Army was evident, and the controversy only worsened as the struggle continued.

During the war the Americans detained by the British Army usually came in one of three categories. First of all, the army often arrested prominent political leaders and detained them for a brief time. Such arrests were employed to give the British Army control over the political process of an area. A second category of persons arrested included the local bureaucrats who proved uncooperative in accepting direction from the Army. Ordinarily the number of civil government figures who were detained was small, but the army did not hesitate to arrest them if they appeared to be, in the view of the army, unreliable. And finally, of course, many persons were apprehended if they were suspected of either resistance or criminal activities. The last category was always the largest in number although it aroused the fewest complaints for obvious reasons.

By the latter part of 1777 enough American civilians had been imprisoned to provoke action by the Continental Congress. The occupation of New York City, and the ensuing campaign of 1776 and 1777, yielded a crowd of captives to his Majesty's troops, and among them was a substantial number of civilians. In 1777, when the Congress formally took a stand on civilian captives, most of the citizens confined by the British Army were located in New York City or on Long Island.[73] On September 6, 1777, Congress went on record by declaring that the British had no right to detain civilians as captives unless they were armed at the time of their capture. Furthermore, Congress asserted that to imprison civilians as captives was contrary to the laws of civilized warfare, and that Great Britain must consider the moral consequences of such barbarous conduct. The Congress did not expect that such a statement would have much effect upon the British, however. So the Congress also advised the states, in the same statement, to inaugurate a program of attempting to supply the imprisoned civilians with food, clothing, and bedding.[74] Congress also cautioned the states to keep strict accounts of their expenditures so the British could be presented with the costs absorbed by the state governments once the war was terminated.

Congress was outraged over the issue of civilian detention for a variety of reasons. Some of its dismay stemmed from very practical considerations, and others were purely for their propaganda value. The September, 1777, declaration was essentially propaganda which was designed to try to raise the morale of the Americans sitting in prison, and to try to put the British Army on the defensive on the whole matter of civilian arrests. Congress failed to point out in its statement that a good many American Loyalists, who were also civilians, had been arrested by the states and jailed. In part, then, the uproar over the civilian arrests was an important propaganda struggle.

In addition to the propaganda reason, Congress was concerned about civilians held captive for two other considerations. First of all, Congress feared that if the arrests continued they would dramatize how little protection the Congress and the state governments could actually provide American non-combatants. In the early and uncertain years of the war, Congress and the states struggled to maintain public support for their policies, and to have their weaknesses regularly emphasized might prove disastrous in their quest for broader esteem among the citizenry. Public apathy toward the Congress and state governments was not uncommon, and the Revolutionary leaders were mindful of that fact. Political considerations also explained some of the anguish that the Congress and the states felt over the detention of private citizens.

Another reason that the Congress and the states were alarmed about the civilian arrests was, indeed, a substantial one. In early May of 1777 the British Army offered to exchange American civilians for British officers held prisoners of war.[75] An offer to swap civilians for officers might at first appear an innocuous one, but Congress refused to consider the proposition. What Congress feared, of course, was that if an agreement was made to exchange civilians for officers, then the British would be encouraged to engage in wholesale arrests of prominent citizens and then offer them for exchange. In effect, the Congress thought the British could manipulate the exchange system, such as it was, by using a sort of blackmail with civilians as the bait. Understandably enough, the Continental Congress, as well as the state governments, cried out bitterly against the civilian arrests. Basically, however, what horrified the Congress and the states most was that there was little they could do to avoid being regularly embarrassed by the arrests of civilians.

Congress' stance on the civilian captives issue did not change appreciably from 1777 until the conclusion of the Revolution. The British Army's detention of American civilians did not diminish as the war went on, and the Congress, on the other hand, never found an effective means to halt the practice or to retaliate successfully.[76] Congress vigorously protested additional arrests but steadfastly refused to negotiate the question with the British authorities. Essentially, Congress turned the question over to the states to solve.

On December 1, 1779, Congress voted not to assume any responsibility for supplying civilians in British prisons with food, clothing, or other items.[77] Congress was not being heartless; it was simply trying to underscore its determination to avoid getting directly involved in the matter of caring for detained non-combatants and to discourage the continuation of arrests. In 1777, and again in 1779, Congress explicitly refused to play any role in the care of civilian captives. The denials of responsibility were motivated by the false hope that the British would cease the arrests once they were convinced the Congress would not exchange officers for civilians.

The civilian captives had to depend on several different sources for their support while in custody. Most of their daily necessities were issued them by the British commissary, but the amount of food and other necessaries they received from their captors was barely adequate. They drew the familiar two-thirds daily food ration, as did the military prisoners, and they also were sporadically given clothing and bedding. But, as was the case with their military brothers, they had to seek outside support as well. Civilian prisoners were permitted to receive gifts of food and other items from friends, relatives, or from their state governments when such supplies became available, but the private citizens suffered a good many hardships because of the lack of proper food and clothing.[78] Until the end of the conflict, the issue of civilian captives remained unresolved, and, in fact, the question became even more complicated in 1780 when Sir Henry Clinton's invading forces seized Charleston, South Carolina.

When Charleston capitulated on May 12, 1780, a garrison of more than 5,400 men was surrendered to the British. Among the Americans who soon found themselves in prison were many prominent civilians who were unfortunate enough to be in the city when its defenses collapsed. Such individuals as Christopher Gadsden, Edward Rutledge, Arthur Middleton, and Thomas Heywood were among those who were quickly arrested when the British occupied the city.[79] Most of the civilians arrested in Charleston, and those detained throughout the Carolinas campaign of 1780-81, were state or municipal government figures, but the anguished outcry from the Congress was, again, a loud one. Congress was greatly annoyed by the renewed arrests. The terms under which Charleston surrendered stipulated that all civil officials, not under arms at the time of surrender, were to be exempt from imprisonment pending their good behavior.[80] Obviously, Congress believed, with some justification, that the British had reneged on their agreement. The British did, indeed, apply a rather loose interpretation to article nine of the surrender document, and many private citizens were jailed in the first weeks of the occupation of Charleston and the outlying area.

As soon as Congress obtained reliable information regarding the arrests of civilians in South Carolina, it directed General Washington to register a formal protest and to inquire why the civilians had been apprehended. As instructed, Washington wrote to Sir Henry Clinton, the Commander in Chief of British forces in America, complaining of the detention of the citizens.[81] He argued again that the arrests violated the rules of civilized warfare, and, furthermore, that the articles under which Charleston had surrendered specifically forbade such action. Clinton promptly replied to Washington's letter. He wrote that the civilians had been jailed because the British Army feared they might lead a conspiracy to destroy the city by fire after it had surrendered.[82] Clinton concluded his letter by stating that Lord Cornwallis, who was in command in South Carolina at that point, was a humane man and that Washington's fears for the safety of the civilian captives were unfounded. Clinton stated that the people held by the British Army would receive fair and just treatment from Cornwallis.[83] General Clinton's response was far from satisfactory in the view of both Congress and General Washington. The British commander refused to debate the issue of the legality of the arrests, and he offered no hint as to whether such arrests would be curtailed. Congress protested while realizing that was about all it could do at that point anyway. Once again, in 1780, the quarrel over the detention of private citizens had intensified.

Special prisons were not established for the civilian prisoners held in the rebellious colonies. Instead, they were lodged any place the British Army found convenient to locate them. Most of the non-military prisoners were detained in New York City prior to the Carolinas campaign of 1780-81. Civilians arrested and imprisoned in New York City were nearly always quartered in the Provost. Persons suspected of spying, supplying intelligence to the rebels, sabotage, inciting resistance, or commission of crimes came under the jurisdiction of Provost Marshall William Cunningham in New York.[84] A few private citizens were incarcerated in New Bridewell or one of the sugar houses, and, on rare occasions, civilians were put aboard one of the prison ships in Wallabout Bay.[85] Elsewhere, as in Charleston, civilians were detained in the public jails and the prison camps, aboard prison ships,[86] or on warships in the harbor.[87] A few private citizens were sent from Charleston to St. Augustine in East Florida and held there for several months before they were released.[88] The normal practice was to hold the civilians for a short time and then to release, exchange, or parole them.

In a few rare instances, American civilians were sent to prisons outside the North American mainland. Cases of American civilians being held on a British possession in the Caribbean were recorded, but they were uncommon. Usually the Americans who were held in the West Indies had been captured at sea and brought there by a British man of war. These captives were normally sent to New York City to await exchange or parole.

An even more uncommon event was the imprisonment of a civilian in Great Britain. A few cases of this type of detention were evident during the Revolution.[89] The practice of sending American civilians from the colonies to prisons in England, on any appreciable scale, did not develop. About the only private American citizens who ended up in prisons in Great Britain were those captured aboard vessels in the Atlantic by British warships which were bound for home. The most famous incident of an American civilian detained in England was that of Henry Laurens.

On August 13, 1780, Henry Laurens, who had been dispatched on a diplomatic mission to the Netherlands by the Continental Congress, departed Philadelphia aboard the brigantine *Mercury*.[90] Off the coast of Newfoundland, the *Mercury* was sighted and pursued by H. M. S. *Vestal*, a twenty-eight gun frigate, and finally captured on September 3, 1780.[91] After Laurens was captured, he was taken to St. Johns, Newfoundland, transferred to another vessel, and sent to England, where he arrived on October 5, 1780.[92] Laurens was taken before the Privy Council for a brief hearing and then committed to close confinement in the Tower of London on October 6, 1780.[93] From October 6, 1780, until December 31, 1781, Laurens resided in the Tower as a captive.[94] While in the Tower of London, he was not mistreated although he did complain regularly of his circumstances there.[95] Finally, Laurens was exchanged for Lord Cornwallis, who was captured at Yorktown in 1781, and was allowed to travel to Paris where he took part in the final phases of the negotiations on the Treaty of Paris.[96] Certainly, the imprisonment of Laurens in the Tower was the most celebrated event involving civilian captives anywhere during the Revolution.

Any attempt to provide an accurate count of the numbers of Americans held prisoners of war by the British Army proves to be an impossible task. A quantity of such documents as staff reports, partial prisoner counts, personal correspondence concerning captives, and other types of papers exists, but when these documents are analyzed the results are unsatisfactory. Enough statistics are available to permit some useful generalizations about the number of men held captive, but a completely accurate census, based on the material now extant, is unlikely. Certainly there are not suffi-cient raw statistics to employ any sophisticated system of analysis beyond an ordinary adding machine.[97]

The first reliable evidence concerning American prisoners of war held in custody by the British Army dates from the Battle of Bunker Hill in 1775. As a result of the engagement, twenty-seven Americans were captured and detained in Boston.[98] While the captives taken by the British at Bunker Hill were few in number, they were important in that the treatment they received would reveal the attitude of the British Army toward its new ad-versaries. Many Patriots feared that the captives might be regarded simply as rebels and quickly punished. Others hoped that the unfortunate men would be regarded as prisoners of war and accorded appropriate treatment. For all practical purposes, the British Army did treat the captives as pris-oners of war without officially declaring them as such. The legal status of Americans captured while in arms remained a murky one until the end of the war, but from the beginning the British dealt with them as though they were a legitimate enemy. Understandably, the British Army was reluctant to commit itself on the issue of the precise status of the captives, since to declare them as prisoners of war might be construed as a recognition of American independence and offer an opportunity for Great Britain's Euro-pean enemies to aid the Revolution. The military skirmishes of 1775 were small and yielded only small numbers of captives. So at the end of 1775 only a handful of Americans were under the jurisdiction of the British Army.

As the war began to escalate in 1776, the number of Americans taken captive by the British began to increase rapidly. During the summer of 1776, approximately three hundred Americans languished in prisons in Quebec. Most of these men were captured during the abortive Canadian campaign which began in late 1775.[99] Then, when General William Howe launched his New York campaign in August of 1776, the number of Amer-icans held captive mounted dramatically. As that offensive neared its end in December of 1776, General Howe reported to Lord George Germain that his newly established military prison system in New York City con-tained a total of 4,430 American officers and enlisted men.[100] Certainly, General Howe's highly successful New York campaign was one of the worst setbacks suffered by the revolutionary forces, and, additionally, it yielded one of the greatest harvests of American captives. So, with more than four thousand Americans held captive by the end of 1776, the pris-oner of war question took on a new meaning and could no longer be ig-nored.

At this point, it might be well to draw attention to some of the problems encountered in trying to make an exact census of the captives held by the British. The most obvious problem is the lack of complete records. The prison commanders compiled voluminous records, but today only tantalizing fragments remain. Other problems also arise when using the fragmentary documents concerning prisoners. Few of the records which still exist are musters. Most of the documents are only numerical counts which do not list the prisoners by name, by regiment, or by any other definite description. Consequently, while the number counts are helpful, such impersonal information cannot be used with any real precision. The problem is simply one of using number counts and having no reliable means to check them against the lists of men who were exchanged, escaped, paroled, or deceased. If the rolls of prisoners which listed the captives by name were available, then it would be possible to compile a nearly complete census. That does not, however, appear possible. Furthermore, when prisoner exchanges were arranged, the normal practice was to list only the number and rank of the men repatriated. Unfortunately, the people of the eighteenth century did not anticipate the greed of later generations for factual information. As a result, about all the student of the prisoner of war question can do is to estimate the numbers of captives held by the British.

During 1777 the numbers of Americans held captive by the British declined noticeably. A natural attrition accounted for part of the reduction. A few prisoners escaped and a good many died. A greater portion of the reduction in the number of American prisoners was promoted by General Howe's decision in 1776 to allow the release of many prisoners or the exchange of cartels of captives.[101] Coupled with the exchange and attrition, Howe's campaign in Pennsylvania in 1777 produced few captives.[102] At the end of 1777 the Board of War reported to the Continental Congress that it estimated that the British held about 1,750 American officers and men in their prisons in Philadelphia and New York.[103] The evidence indicates, therefore, that the number of Americans held by the British Army appears to have declined by better than fifty percent during the course of events in 1777.

The year of 1778, basically, was an uneventful one militarily. General Henry Clinton succeeded William Howe as Commander in Chief of British forces, and shortly thereafter the war slowed down. The only important military clash between the American and British forces to take place in the northern colonies occurred at Monmouth, New Jersey, in June of 1778. The battle was an indicisive conflict and produced few captives on either side. Once Clinton was safely ensconced in New York City, he refused to offer significant battle for the rest of the year. So few opportunities to make prisoners of war presented themselves to Clinton's immediate command. About the only other important military operation of 1778 which produced many prisoners was the invasion of Savannah, Georgia, by a British force led by Lieutenant Colonel Archibald Campbell. Campbell reported to General Clinton on December 29, 1778, that he had 453 American officers and men confined as prisoners of war.[104]

Meanwhile, in New York City, the British Army claimed to have 404 Americans in prisons or on parole.[105] The lull in military activity plus the exchange, paroles, escapes, and deaths of American personnel had reduced the total of captives under the jurisdiction of the British Army to 857. It appears, from the sparse evidence available, that the number of men detained by the British at the end of 1778 had declined to about twenty percent of the total of 1776. The figure had dwindled from a high of 4,430 to 857 by the end of 1778.

The steady decline in the number of Americans held by the British Army continued in 1779. Military activity on the part of the British Army was limited in 1779, and few captives were taken that year. The frontiers of Virginia, New York, and Pennsylvania were vexed with Indian troubles, but few of the captives from the raids there reached British prisons. The net result was, of course, that the sum of Americans held by the army continued to decrease. At this point, colonial prisoners were largely concentrated in New York City. On March 1, 1779, Joshua Loring, the Commissary General of Prisoners, informed General Clinton that he had 286 captives under his care.[106] By midsummer of 1779 Loring's weekly reports indicated that the number of captives had risen to 464.[107] For the balance of 1779 the total of American captives never exceeded six hundred.

In early 1780 a few minor skirmishes in the New York City vicinity, such as those at Marrineck, Elizabethtown, Newark, and Phillip's Manor, produced a few captives, and on February 22, 1780, Loring listed a total of 729 inmates in his prisons.[108] Then the number of men detained in New York stabilized. In April of 1780 Loring reported he had 702 men under his control.[109] Congress estimated on August 19, 1780, that approximately 720 Americans were still in the British prisons in New York City and on Long Island.[110] While there was a slight increase in the number of men held by the British, it was not a dramatic one. The major military event of 1780 was the invasion of Charleston, South Carolina. This campaign yielded a great many captives.

The South Carolina campaign of 1780 provided captives on a scale reminiscent of 1776. When Charleston capitulated in 1780, more than 5,400 American troops surrendered to General Clinton's forces. Clinton promptly paroled most of the state militia and then dispatched the remaining militia and the Continental troops to hurriedly improvised prisons. By August of 1780, a total of 2,084 American officers and men were listed as inmates of the South Carolina military prison system.[111] More prisoners were added to the prison camps by such British victories in 1780 as the Battles of Camden, Waxhaws, and others which finally raised the total to 3,039.[112] By the end of 1780 the sum of Americans held captive in New York and in the South would have been about 3,700.[113] From this point, the number of Americans detained began to dwindle again. At the peak point, the British Army never formally detained more than about 4,500 men. And that was in 1776.

After the defeat of Lord Cornwallis at Yorktown in 1781, prisoner exchanges were increased, and by early 1782 only a handful of Americans remained in captivity in New York and a few hundred awaited exchange at Charleston.[114] The number of Americans held by the British Army at any one time was never great.

FOOTNOTES

[1] Lord Germain to Lords of the Admiralty, December 27, 1775. Headquarters Papers of the British Army in America, Microfilm copy, Reel 2A, Document 102. Cited hereafter as BHQP.

[2] Peter Force, ed., *American Archives*, 5th Series, (Washington, D. C., 1837-1853), II, 190, 252-53. Cited hereafter Force, *American Archives*. BHQP, Reel 3A, Document 853, George Washington to Lieutenant General Haldimand, August 30, 1780, Fitzpatrick, *Writings of Washington*, XIX, 473.

[3] Major Return Meigs to George Washington, July 25, 1776, Sparks, *Correspondence*, I, 265.

[4] Charles I. Bushnell, ed., *The Narrative of John Blatchford* (New York, 1865), 10, 73n. Cited hereafter Bushnell, *Narrative of Blatchford.*

[5] Board of War Report, January 21, 1778, Worthington C. Ford, ed., *The Journals of the Continental Congress* (Washington, D. C. 1904-1937), X, 74. Cited hereafter as JCC.

[6] General Prevost to General Howe, April 5, 1778, BHQP, Reel 4, Document 1069.

[7] John Mathews to George Washington, May 6, 1781, E. C. Burnett, ed., *Letters of the Members of the Continental Congress* (Washington, D. C., 1921-1938), VI, 14-15. Cited hereafter Burnett, *Letters.* Christopher Gadsden to George Washington, August 10, 1781, Sparks, *Correspondence*, III, 376. Papers of the Continental Congress, Microfilm copy, Roll 177, Item

489, 158. Cited hereafter as PCC.

[8] Banastre, Tarleton, *A History of the Campaigns of 1780 and 1781 in the Southern Provinces of North America* (New York, 1968), 53, 61, 63. Cited hereafter Tarleton, *History of the Campaign in the Southern Provinces.* Anthony Allaire, *Diary of Lieutenant Anthony Allaire* (New York, 1968), 15.

[9] Thomas Jefferson to Benjamin Harrison, February 7, 1781, Julian P. Boyd, ed., *The Papers of Thomas Jefferson* (Princeton, 1950-), IV, 550. Cited hereafter as Boyd, *Papers of Jefferson.* PCC, Roll 177, Item 158, 509, 513-14, 525.

[10] President of Congress to George Washington, February 7, 1780, Burnett, *Letters*, V, 25.

[11] Benjamin Franklin to Lord Stormont, April 23, 1777, Albert H. Smyth, ed., *The Writings of Benjamin Franklin* (New York, 1905-1907), VII, 36-37. Benjamin Franklin to M. De Sartine, May 8, 1779, *ibid.*, VIII, 512. Cited hereafter as Smyth, *Writings of Franklin.*

[12] PCC, Roll 177, Item 19, 425.

[13] Charles Thomson, Notes on Debates, August 28, 1782, Burnett, *Letters*, VI, 460. Benjamin Franklin to William Hodgson, March 31, 1782, Smyth, *Writings of Franklin*, VIII, 409.

[14] John Pintard, "The Old Jail," *The New York Mirror*, September 10, 1831, 1. Eugene L. Armbruster, *The Wallabout Prison Ships, 1776-1783* (New York, 1920), 29. Cited hereafter Armbruster, *Prison Ships.*

[15] *Ibid.*

[16] Ethan Allen, *Allen's Captivity, being a Narrative of Colonel Ethan Allen* (Boston, 1845), 123. Cited hereafter as Allen, *Narrative.*

[17] Returns of the Provost, July 8, 1778, June 1, 1779, November 1, 1779, November 29, 1779, December 6, 1779, June 19, 1780, June 30, 1780, August 27, 1781, Sir Henry Clinton Papers, William L. Clements Library, Ann Arbor, Michigan. Cited hereafter as Clinton Papers.

[18] *Ibid.*

[19] Elias Boudinot to H. H. Ferguson, April 20, 1778, Elias Boudinot Papers, The Historical Society of Pennsylvania, Philadelphia, Pennsylvania. Cited hereafter as Boudinot Papers. Cunningham came to America in 1774, and was later humiliated by the Sons of Liberty when they forced him to kiss a liberty pole which had been erected in New York City. Most writers think his hostility toward American prisoners was, in part, motivated by this incident. In 1791, Cunningham was executed by the British Army for stealing money from the Board of Ordnance accounts. Henry Onderdonck, *Revolutionary Incidents of Suffolk and King's Counties; With an Account of the Battle of Long Island and the Prison-Ships at New York* (New York,

1849), 245-247. Cited hereafter as Onderdonck, *Revolutionary Incidents*. Richard H. Amerman, "Treatment of American Prisoners During the Revolution," *New Jersey Historical Society Proceedings*, LXXVIII (1960), 266-268.

[20] Onderdonck, *Revolutionary Incidents*, 210.

[21] Sir William Howe to Lord George Germain, December 13, 1776, Force, *American Archives*, III, 1054-58.

[22] Danske Dandridge, *American Prisoners of the Revolution* (Baltimore, 1967), 25. Cited hereafter as Dandridge, *American Prisoners*. As many as 800 men may have been placed in New Bridewell at the end of 1776, Force, *American Archives*, III, 76.

[23] Ambrose Serle, *American Journal of Ambrose Serle, 1776-1778* (San Marino, 1940), 305. Frank Moore, ed., *Diary of the American Revolution* (New York, 1860), I, 374. Cited hereafter as Moore, *Diary*.

[24] Dandridge, *American Prisoners*, 24-25.

[25] *Ibid.*, 25-26.

[26] Board of War Report, January 21, 1778, JCC, X, 74. Onderdonck, *Revolutionary Incidents*, 207-8.

[27] Dandridge, *American Prisoners*, 25-26. For example, beginning in 1778, after the other sugar house prisons were closed the Liberty Street prison contained 141 men on December 26, 1778, Mackenzie Papers. Weekly Returns of Prisoners, June 28, 1779, and April 22, 1781, Clinton Papers.

[28] Henry Stiles, ed., *Letters From The Prisons and Prison-Ships* (New York, 1865), 7-11. Cited hereafter as Stiles, *Letters*. Hiram Stone, "The Experiences of a Prisoner in the American Revolution," *The Journal of American History*, II (1908), 527-29.

[29] Onderdonck, *Revolutionary Incidents*, 207-10.

[30] Dandridge, *American Prisoners*, 103. David L. Sterling, ed., "Prisoners of War in New York: A Report by Elias Boudinot," *William and Mary Quarterly*, Third Series, XIII (1956), 380. Cited hereafter as Sterling, "American Prisoners."

[31] *Ibid.* Elias Boudinot was appointed Commissary General of Prisoners on June 6, 1777, by the Continental Congress. JCC, VIII, 422. As Commissary General of Prisoners, Boudinot was allowed to visit New York City to inspect the prisons and hospitals where American troops were detained. Boudinot resigned his post on April 20, 1778. PCC, Roll 72, Item 59, 52.

[32] Dandridge, *American Prisoners*, 100-104. PCC, Roll 91, Item 78, 353. Elias Boudinot, *Journal or Historical Recollections of American Events During the Revolutionary War* (Philadelphia, 1894), 18-19. Cited hereafter as Boudinot, *Journal*.

[33] W. H. W. Sabine, ed., *The New York Diary of Lieutenant Jabez Fitch* (New York, 1954), 34-35. Cited hereafter as Sabine, *Diary of Fitch*. Dandridge, *American Prisoners*, 29.

[34] Howard H. Peckham, ed., *Memoirs of the Life of John Adlum in the Revolutionary War* (Chicago, 1968), 89-90. Cited hereafter as Peckham, *Memoirs of Adlum.*

[35] *Ibid.*, 87-88, 100-104, 127-28, 138. Sabine, *Diary of Fitch*, 54-104. Worthington C. Ford, ed., "British and American Prisoners of War, 1778," *The Pennsylvania Magazine of History and Biography*, XVII (1895), 159-74, 316-24. Onderdonck, *Revolutionary Incidents*, 213.

[36] Peckham, *Memoirs of Adlum*, 87-88, 100, 127-28. Sabine, *Diary of Fitch*, 65-103. Fitch later moved to Long Island. Adlum was not an officer but he was released from New Bridewell when Colonel Robert Magaw of Pennsylvania asked for him and Adlum became an orderly to Colonel Magaw.

[37] PCC, Roll 91, Item 78, 353. Charles A. Huguenin, "Ethan Allen, Parolee On Long Island," *Vermont History*, XXV (1907), 105-09.

[38] Helen Jordan, ed., "Colonel Elias Boudinot in New York City, February, 1778," *The Pennsylvania Magazine of History and Biography*, XXIV (1900), 456-57.

[39] Caesar Rodney to John Dickinson, April 17, 1779, and Caesar Rodney to General Assembly, January 25, 1781, George H. Ryder, ed., *Letters to and from Caesar Rodney, 1756-1784* (Philadelphia, 1933), 298-395. Cited hereafter as Ryder, *Letters to Rodney.*

[40] George Washington to Lieutenant General Thomas Gage, August 11, 1775, Fitzpatrick, *Writings of Washington*, III, 416. Washington's protests were duly noted in London. William Eden to Lord George Germain, September 18, 1775, Sackville-Germain Papers, William L. Clements Library, Ann Arbor, Michigan. Cited hereafter as Sackville-Germain Papers. ·

[41] General Gage to George Washington, August 13, 1775, General Thomas Gage Papers, William L. Clements Library, Ann Arbor, Michigan. Cited hereafter as Gage Papers.

[42] Elias Cornelius, *Journal of Dr. Elias Cornelius* (New York, 1902), 5. Cited hereafter as Cornelius, *Journal.* Peckham, *Memoirs of Adlum,* 74. Sabine, *Diary of Fitch*, 33.

[43] Cornelius, *Journal*, 5. George Washington to Samuel Chase, February 5, 1777, Fitzpatrick, *Writings of Washington*, VII, 108.

[44] Cornelius, *Journal*, 6.

[45] Lorenzo Sabine, ed., *Biographical Sketches of Loyalists of the American Revolution with an Historical Essay* (Port Washington, New York, 1966), II, 27-28. Cited hereafter as Sabine, *Sketches.*

[46] There were five Commissary Generals who had authority over prisoners in America. In addition to Loring, who handled American army personnel, there was David Sproat who handled naval prisoners. The other three had little to do with the American captives and will not be discussed. The three were the Commissary Generals for French, Spanish, and Dutch prisoners. Thomas Jones, *History of New York During the Revolutionary War* edited by Thomas Floyd de Lancey (New York, 1879), I, 351-52. Cited hereafter as Jones, *History of New York.*

[47] Sabine, *Sketches*, II, 27-28. Sabine, *Diary of Fitch*, 36n-37n. Jones, *History of New York*, I, 351.

[48] *Ibid.*

[49] PCC, Roll 72, Item 59, 47.

[50] George Washington to Robert Morris, George Clymer, and George Walton, January 12, 1777, Fitzpatrick, *Writings of Washington*, VI, 503-04.

[51] General Howe to George Washington, April 21, 1777, BHQP, Reel 3, Document 500.

[52] General Howe to George Washington, January 19, 1778, *ibid.*, Reel 3A, Document 896.

[53] *Ibid.*

[54] For an interesting discussion of the British Army policy of provisioning its men see John Shy, *Toward Lexington, The Role of the British Army in the Coming of the Revolution* (Princeton, New Jersey, 1965), 27, 110, 119-20, 175, 240, 331-32, 339. In peacetime a regular deduction was made from the soldier's pay to defray the cost of his rations. In wartime, his rations were free.

[55] *Ibid.* A later chapter will deal in detail with the means employed to supplement the captives' rations.

[56] Jonathan Gillett to Elizabeth Gillett, December 12, 1776, Stiles, *Letters*, II, 38. Charles I. Bushnell, ed., *A Narrative of the Life of Levi Hanford, A Soldier of the Revolution* (New York, 1863), 19. Cited hereafter as Bushnell, *Narrative of Hanford.*

[57] General Howe to George Washington, December 12, 1776, BHQP, Reel 3, Document 340.

[58] Sabine, *Diary of Fitch*, 159. Peckham, *Memoirs of Adlum*, 90n. Enclosure to Sir Henry Clinton, July 1, 1780, Clinton Papers.

[59] JCC, IX, 1036-37, *ibid.*, XVI, 15, 381. Elias Boudinot to Captain Mackenzie, November 25, 1777, BHQP, Reel 3A, Document 758. Elias Boudinot Ledger, 1760-1814, New York Public Library, 70. Cited hereafter as Boudinot Ledger. John S. Littell, ed., *Memoirs of His Own Time with Reminiscences of the Men and Events of the Revolution by Alexander Graydon* (Philadelphia, 1846), 247. Cited hereafter as Littell, *Memoirs*

of Graydon.

[60] Moore, *Diary*, I, 374.

[61] John Thatcher, *A Military Journal during the American Revolutionary War* (Boston, 1823), 89-91. Cited hereafter as Thatcher, *Journal*. Onderdonck, *Revolutionary Incidents*, 220-25. PCC, Roll 91, Item 78, 211-12, 353. Peckham, *Memoirs of Adlum*, 99.

[62] PCC, Roll 91, Item 78, 353.

[63] Sabine, *Diary of Fitch*, 188.

[64] Dandridge, *American Prisoners*, 119.

[65] Board of War to Commissary General of Prisoners, June 24, 1777, PCC, Roll 25, Item 28, 37-38. Boudinot, *Journal*, 10, 58-59. Lewis Pintard to Elias Boudinot, May 5, 1777, Boudinot Papers. Elias Boudinot to Captain Mackenzie, no date, BHQP, Reel 3A, Document 758.

[66] Benjamin Rush to John Adams, October 1, 1777, L.H. Butterfield ed., *Letters of Benjamin Rush* (Princeton, New Jersey, 1951), I, 244-45. Cited hereafter as Butterfield, *Letters of Rush,* Dandridge, *American Prisoners*, 102-4.

[67] Dandridge, *American Prisoners*, 102. Sidney Barclay, ed., *Personal Recollections of the American Revolution, A Private Journal Prepared from Authentic Records by Lydia Minturn Post* (Port Washington, New York, 1970), 26-33. Cited hereafter as Barclay, *Recollections of Lydia Post.* George Washington Lafayette, ed., *Memoirs, Correspondence and Manuscripts of General Lafayette* (London, 1837), 24. Cited hereafter as Lafayette, *Memoirs.*

[68] General Howe to George Washington, April 21, 1777, BHQP, Reel 3, Document 500. Dandridge, *American Prisoners*, 75-76, 86.

[69] Sterling, "American Prisoners," 380.

[70] Howe admitted a high death rate among the prisoners but he thought it to be unavoidable. General Howe to George Washington, April 21, 1777, BHQP, Reel 3, Document 500. Robert Morris, George Clymer, and George Walton to George Washington, January 1, 1777, Sparks, *Correspondence,* I, 324-26.

[71] PCC, Roll 72, Item 59, 51. JCC, X, 203. Henry Laurens to George Washington, November 19, 1777, Burnett, *Letters*, II, 559-60. Elias Boudinot to George Washington, May 13, 1778, Sparks, *Correspondence*, II, 122-23. C. J. Hoadly and L. W. Larabee, eds., *Public Records of the State of Connecticut, 1776-1796* (Hartford, 1894-1951), II, 185. Cited hereafter as Hoadly and Larabee, *Public Records of Connecticut.*

[72] The British Army did try to establish law and order in all the areas under its control. Unfortunately, the army's success was limited. One of the more fascinating accounts of life in an occupied zone was written by Lydia

Minturn Post. Mrs. Post's husband was an officer in the Revolutionary forces, and she spent the war living on their farm on Long Island. Among the many useful observations in her journal, Mrs. Post recorded the examples of lawlessness which prevailed in her neighborhood during the war. Barclay, *Recollections of Lydia Post*, 84-86, 89-92, 104-8, 109-40, 150-51, 157-59, 163-67. Mrs. Post's journal gives some insight into the terrors of living in an occupied area.

[73]PCC, Roll 35, Item 28, 55. Civilians were allowed to seek arrangements in private homes on Long Island. They were paroled, but with the normal restrictions of travel.

[74]*Ibid.*

[75]George Washington to Colonel David Forman, May 15, 1777, Fitzpatrick, *Writings of Washington*, VIII, 66-67.

[76]Committee of Congress to George Washington, March 15, 1779, Burnett, *Letters*, IV, 104-5. George Washington to Abraham Skinner, August 8, 1781, Fitzpatrick, *Writings of Washington*, XXII, 479. Thomas Jefferson to General Nelson, January 20, 1781, H. R. McIlwaine, ed., *Official Letters of the Governors of the State of Virginia* (Richmond, 1926-1929), II, 296. Cited hereafter as McIlwaine, *Letters.*

[77]PCC, Roll 35, Item 28, 59.

[78]Hoadly and Larabee, *Public Records of Connecticut*, II, 299-300. George Washington to William Howe, January 20, 1778, Fitzpatrick, *Writings of Washington*, X, 324. George Washington to William Duane, May 3, 1779, *ibid.*, XIV, 477. George Washington to John Beatty, August 18, 1779, *ibid.*, XVI, 131. Henry Laurens to Benjamin Lincoln, July 17, 1779, Burnett, *Letters*, IV, 322. James Duane to George Washington, May 17, 1779, *ibid.*, 216-17.

[79]President of Congress to Nathanael Greene, September 24, 1780, Burnett, *Letters*, V, 388. George Washington to James Cannon, September 3, 1780, Fitzpatrick, *Writings of Washington*, XIX, 492.

[80]Articles of Capitulation of Charleston South Carolina, Tarleton, *History of the Campaign in the Southern Provinces*, 63. See article nine for the terms of the surrender regarding civilians.

[81]George Washington to Sir Henry Clinton, October 6, 1780, Fitzpatrick, *Writings of Washington*, XX, 128. George Washington to Sir Henry Clinton, October 6, 1780, BHQP, Reel 8, Document 3058. PCC, Roll 72, Item 59, 60.

[82]Sir Henry Clinton to George Washington, October 9, 1780, BHQP, Reel 9, Document 3061.

[83]*Ibid.*

[84]Report of Prisoners in the Provost, July 7, 1778, June 1, 1779, No-

vember 1, 1779, November 8, 1779, November 29, 1779, December 13, 1779, April 30, 1780, June 30, 1780, and April 15, 1782, Clinton Papers.

[85] George Washington to Richard, Lord Howe, May 10, 1778, Fitzpatrick, *Writings of Washington*, XI, 368-69. George Washington to Governor Nicholas Cooke, May 26, 1778, *ibid.*, 455. Hoadly and Larabee, *Public Records of Connecticut*, II, 299-300.

[86] PCC, Roll 72, Item 59, 60. JCC, XVII, 851.

[87] Sir Henry Clinton to George Washington, October 9, 1780, BHQP, Reel 9, Document 3061. President of Congress to Nathanael Greene, September 24, 1780, Burnett, *Letters*, V, 388.

[88] JCC, XX, 621. John Mathews to Nathanael Greene, August 14, 1781, Burnett, *Letters*, VI, 181. William Moultrie to J. Mathews, March 21, 1781, PCC, Roll 177, Item 158, 489.

[89] James Lovell to Benjamin Franklin, May 9, 1781, Burnett, *Letters*, VI, 85.

[90] Henry Laurens, "Narrative of his Capture and of his confinement in the Tower of London etc., 1780, 1781, 1782," *South Carolina Historical Collections*, I (1857), 18-19.

[91] *Ibid.*, 20.

[92] *Ibid.*, 20-23.

[93] *Ibid.*, 25-26.

[94] *Ibid.*, 60.

[95] Benjamin Franklin to Samuel Huntington, November 3, 1780, Smyth, *Writings of Franklin*, VIII, 185.

[96] General Washington to Sir Guy Carleton July 30, 1782, and Sir Guy Carleton and Rear Admiral Digby to George Washington, August 2, 1782, Charles Ross, ed., *Correspondence of Charles, First Marquis Cornwallis* (London, 1859), I, 140.

[97] For additional insight to the problem of dealing with the figures on prisoners of war see Metzger, *The Prisoner in the American Revolution* (Chicago, 1971), 206. Cited hereafter as Metzger, *Prisoner in the Revolution*.

[98] Report on Prisoners taken in the Battle of Bunker Hill, June 17, 1775, Mackenzie Papers.

[99] Major Return Meigs to George Washington, July 25, 1776, Sparks, *Correspondence*, I, 265.

[100] Sir William Howe to Lord George Germain, December 3, 1776, Force, *American Archives*, III, 1054-58. Also see Onderdonck, *Revolutionary Incidents*, 212.

[101] Moore, *Diary*, I, 374, 377. American and British miliary authorities regularly referred to groups of prisoners involved in exchanges as cartels.

[102] According to official records only 315 men captured at Brandywine

reached British prisons. Report of Prisoners taken at the Battle of Brandywine on September 11, 1777, Mackenzie Papers. The peak number of men held captive in Philadelphia was probably 790.

[103] Board of War Report, JCC, X, 74.

[104] Return of Prisoners of War taken in action 29 December 1778 by His Majesty's Forces under the command of Lt. Col. Archibald Campbell of the 71st Regiment, Clinton Papers.

[105] General State of Prisoners, New York, December 26, 1778, Mackenzie Papers.

[106] Weekly Report of Prisoners, March 1, 1779, Clinton Papers.

[107] Weekly Report of Prisoners, June 28, 1779, Clinton Papers. According to this report, of the 464 men incarcerated at least 235 were officers. Exchanges for officers were always more complicated and slower to be completed.

[108] Return of Prisoners, February 22, 1780, Clinton Papers. List of Prisoners taken at Marrineck, January 18, 1780, List of Rebel Prisoners taken at Elizabethtown, New Jersey, January 25, 1780, List of Prisoners taken at Newark, January 26, 1780, List of Rebel Prisoners taken at Phillips' Manor, February 3, 1780, Mackenzie Papers.

[109] Joshua Loring to John André, April 1, 1780, Clinton Papers.

[110] Board of War Report, August 19, 1780. JCC, XVII, 753.

[111] List of Continental Prisoners of War, Charleston, South Carolina, August 7, 1780, Mackenzie Papers.

[112] Return of Prisoners taken Battle of Camden, August 16, 1780, and Return of Prisoners taken by the Troops under the command of Lt. Col. Tarleton in the action at Catawba Ford, August 18, 1780, Mackenzie Papers.

[113] JCC, XVII, 753.

[114] General Return of Prisoners, April 22, 1781, Weekly State of Provost, April 15, 1782, Clinton Papers. Archibald Lytle to Ichabod Burnet, October 29, 1782, Return of the Officers of the Infantry of the Virginia Line that have been made prisoners in the Southern Department, October 27, 1782, and a list of the Maryland and Delaware Lines who were Prisoners in the Southern Department, Nathanael Greene Papers, William L. Clements Library, Ann Arbor, Michigan. Cited hereafter as Greene Papers.

chapter three

Prisoners of the British Navy

A casual reader of the works on the American Revolution frequently encounters descriptions of how the British treated captured American seamen. Most accounts of the Revolution usually mention the British prison ships and the suffering of the men lodged aboard them, while ignoring any further discussion of the whole naval prisoner of war issue. The prison ships, and the conditions the inmates aboard them endured, made an indelible impression upon all those who witnessed their existence and upon later generations. There can be little doubt that the prison ships were the most notorious aspect of the Revolution in regard to prisoners of war.

Confinement in a prison ship was a comparatively dramatic fate which aroused an indignation among our Revolutionary forefathers that was kept alive by the extremely nationalistic accounts of the war written in the nineteenth and early twentieth centuries. The men who spent time in these prison ships did suffer mightily, but their hardships were only a part of the story of naval prisoners of war who, in turn, are a segment of the whole unhappy episode for both navy and army personnel.

In addition to the use of prison ships to confine captured American seamen, the British also transported sizable numbers of American sailors to prisons outside the colonies — chiefly to Great Britain. This practice of imprisoning American naval personnel abroad has received scant attention. A few diaries of prisoners who spent some time in England or elsewhere have been published, but little serious study of the topic has appeared. Throughout the war the greater number of Americans held captive by the Royal Navy was located in America or in Great Britain. Captured Americans were, however, to be found in prisons or aboard prison ships in the West Indies or just about any place British warships were on patrol.

Many Americans spent weeks aboard a British man-of-war after their capture before they were finally transferred to a more permanent prison to await exchange. A British warship on patrol had a duty to fulfill, and if Americans were seized they stayed on board the vessel until the patrol was completed or until they could be sent aboard another vessel which could carry them to a prison or a prison ship. Consequently, many Americans spent a good deal of time in men-of-war too busy to take them into port where the captives could be quartered more readily. In most ways the history of the American seamen as prisoners of war is a much more complicated one than that of the army personnel, because the places of their confinement were much more varied, scattered, and under the jurisdiction of an incredible number of different persons and agencies.

The advent of the prison ship was an early one, and it came at New York City. In the latter part of October, 1776, a large transport named the *Whitby* was anchored in Wallabout Bay near Remsen's Mill on Long Island across from New York City and converted into a prison to hold a part of the flood of prisoners General William Howe's successful New York campaign produced.[1]

Soon after the decrepit *Whitby* began service as a prison, several other vessels also were fitted out for similar duty. At first the prison ships were used to detain army personnel as well as naval captives, until sufficient facilities were provided in New York City and on Long Island for army prisoners. It was not until 1777 that prison ships were used almost exclusively as prisons for American seamen. After the British occupied New York City in the autumn of 1776, a number of old vessels which had carried grain and cattle to America and a few aged, obsolete warships were designated to serve as prisons.[2] Most of the vessels which became prisons had outlived their usefulness, and they were put to the only function left for them to carry out. The majority of the prison vessels were anchored in Wallabout Bay across from New York City on Long Island, which today is the site of the New York Naval Shipyard. A few of the prison ships were also anchored in the Hudson River and the East River,[3] but they were finally moved to Wallabout Bay to concentrate the prison fleet to facilitate easier administration and to try to make escape from the river fleet more difficult for their inmates.

The list of the prison and hospital ships used in the New York City area and elsewhere from 1776 to 1782 is a rather imposing one. Prison ships, as mentioned earlier, were the chief means employed to detain American naval personnel, although the first several months of the occupation of

New York a good many army troops were placed aboard them until a regular prison system was established to control non-naval captives. Two types of duty were assigned to the vessels. The majority of the ships were prisons. A smaller number of the prison fleet served as hospitals to care for the captives who were wounded at the time they were captured or to tend to those inmates of the prison hulks who fell ill during their captivity. Naval prisoners who were injured or ill from causes not associated with capture or imprisonment were also placed aboard the floating hospitals.

By far and away, the most infamous of the prison ships was the *Jersey*.[4] The *Jersey* is nearly always mentioned when writers allude to the British practice of converting old vessels into prisons, but there were many more used for the same purpose. Including the *Jersey*, there is solid evidence of the existence of at least twenty-six ships which were converted into prisons between 1776 and 1782. The names of the ships which the records show as having served as prisons were: *John, Glasgow, Whitby, Jersey, Preston, Good Intent, Good Hope, Prince of Wales, Grovnor, Falmouth, Strombolo, Lord Dunlace, Scorpion, Judith, Myrtle, Felicity, Chatham, Kitty, Frederick, Woodlands, Scheldt,* and *Clyde*.[5] In addition to these prison ships, three vessels served as hospitals to the New York prison fleet. They were the *Hunter, Perserverance,* and *Bristol Packet*.[6] All of the foregoing vessels saw service at one time or another in the New York vicinity.

There is evidence of other prison ships in use at other places. After the fall of Charleston, South Carolina, in 1780, two ships named *Torbay* and *Pack-Horse* were anchored in Charleston harbor and employed as prisons.[7] Additionally, a ship named the *Peter* was stationed at St. Lucia in the West Indies to handle naval prisoners too.[8] Very little information about the *Torbay, Pack-Horse,* and *Peter* appears to have survived, but the fragments of evidence indicate they were similar in appearance and function to the more famous prison ships of New York.

The records establish, therefore, that the British Navy commissioned at least twenty-six ships to serve as prisons and three vessels to serve as hospitals which were stationed in three locations. The vast majority of them were to be found at New York City, and the others were located at Charleston and St. Lucia.

A prison ship was an awesome sight to behold. The normal practice at New York City, where most of the floating prisons were employed, was to move an obsolete warship or an aging merchantman to a secure but isolated anchorage where it could be converted to a prison. A few of the prison vessels, as mentioned before, were anchored in the Hudson and East Rivers, but most of them were situated in Wallabout Bay across from New

York City on Long Island. The prime consideration was that the bay was conveniently located, in relation to New York City, for easy access to the hulks for administrative purposes. Furthermore, Wallabout Bay, while it was close to the city, was located in such a fashion that the prison fleet riding at anchor there presented little hazard to the heavy harbor traffic. And finally, the bay was large enough that men who tried to escape the prisons had first to cross an expanse of water and mud flats which would make their attempts much more difficult, if not impossible. Then, if a prisoner managed to negotiate the bay somehow, he still had several water-ways and heavily populated areas to pass in trying to reach freedom in New Jersey or New England. So from the security standpoint Wallabout Bay had its merits. At least the British Navy thought so. Escape from the Wallabout fleet was not impossible, but it required a tremendous effort by a determined man.

A prison ship was not difficult to identify. Once a vessel was fitted out to serve as a prison the outward appearance betrayed its function. The first step toward converting a vessel into a prison, after she was moored at her station, was to remove all her usable fittings. A prison hulk was normally stripped of her rudder, masts, spars, rigging, and other equipment which was not needed by a ship that would never put out to sea again. Aside from the hull, about all that remained of the exterior of the vessel was the flagstaff, bowsprit, and a spar amidship which was used as a derrick to hoist supplies aboard. For example, the *Jersey*, which was a widely re-nowned prison, was once a stately sixty-four gun warship which had been stripped of all her masts, spars, rigging, and ordnance.[9] The *Jersey* was re-duced to an ugly, somber hulk. Her gun ports were sealed, and along the hull two tiers of holes twenty inches square and ten feet apart had been cut. These openings were the only source of light and ventilation for the prisoners.[10] The prisoners were quartered below, and the crew and guard lived in the aft section of the vessel. All the hatches except one were sealed. The aft hatch was the only means to the waist of the ship, and near the hatch a barricade was constructed. From behind this barricade the guard detail could control access to the quarterdeck. A heavy grate was placed over the hatch at night to help the guard control the inmates. Then, on days of good weather, the grate was removed and prisoners were allowed to come topside to enjoy the sun, fresh air, and exercise. The barricade located at the break of the quarterdeck was always manned by armed sen-tries who could rake the hatchway or deck with gunfire if the prisoners became unruly.[11] Details regarding such arrangements on prison hulks varied slightly due to the differences of the vessels which composed the fleet, but basically the pattern was the same among them.

On board a prison ship there were two detachments of men who were responsible for operating the prison. A crew consisting of a captain, two mates, steward, cook, and twelve sailors saw to the needs of the vessel.[12] They kept the ship repaired, loaded provisions and water aboard, and generally did little else. Contact between the prisoners and the permanent crew was infrequent. About the only time the crew and the prisoners were together was during work details when prisoners were recruited to help. Isolating the crew from the captives as much as possible was standard practice. The second detachment of men aboard the prison hulk were the guards. A guard detail was normally composed of an officer and thirty men who were relieved each week by a fresh party of guards.[13] Guard detachments were usually British or German soldiers, although Loyalist detachments were sometimes used. Apparently, the inmates preferred German guard details as they were inclined to be less severe in the performance of their duties. The Loyalists, of course, were most despised by the prisoners.[14] So under normal circumstances a prison ship was manned by a combined force of about fifty men.

Life aboard the prison ships was a difficult one for their inmates. A prison ship was a gloomy-looking thing from the outside, but its ominous appearance could not reveal the squalor the captives in the ship endured. Inside the stern-looking prison, the prisoners lived a life of subtle agony. The basic problem all captives contended with was the overcrowded conditions common among the prison ships.[15] Too many people packed into too little space was the cause of much of the day-to-day discomfort the prisoners suffered. Most of each twenty-four hour period the prisoners were confined between decks. Each day small groups of the inmates were allowed topside for brief periods, but the escape from the desperately crowded conditions was infrequent for each man. At sundown the men were all sent below, and then the next morning, on rotating order, they were permitted to return to the fresh air again. In a heavily populated vessel a prisoner might wait for several days until his turn to go topside came again.

Confining several hundred men into a small area presented a number of obvious problems. Living with no privacy usually brought out the quarrelsome aspect of an inmate's personality, which meant that the hostility among the prisoners for each other was open and active.[16] Some of the horror of the prisoners' life was due in part to men who broke down under the strain of the routine and became dangerous. The guards made no effort to try to sort out the prisoners who became emotionally unbalanced and to isolate them from the rest of the captives. All too often the deranged individual had to commit some especially violent act before he was taken from among the other prisoners. By that time, it was, of course, too late for the victim.

The crowded conditions aboard the prison ships promoted the predictable host of problems. Several hundred men packed into a vessel soon became weary of the foul, dead air they had to breathe. Poor ventilation in a prison ship was commonplace, and in the summer months the stench associated with the hulks was especially oppressive. In addition to poor ventilation, there was little provision for bathing and sanitary facilities. In fact, bathing was almost unknown, and the sanitary facilities usually consisted of a number of wooden tubs which were called the latrine. Consequently, the ship reeked of the odor of human waste. Once each day the tubs were carried topside and emptied over the side, but the horrible stench lingered on between decks.[17]

To compound the misery of the captives aboard the prison ships, they usually lacked adequate clothing and bedding.[18] Normally, the prisoners had to make do with whatever garments and bedding they possessed when they were captured, until they could somehow obtain replacements. Since the British never established a standard policy of periodically issuing clothing, bedding, and other necessaries to the naval prisoners of war, a prisoner had to barter, buy, or steal what he needed. About the only bedding and clothing from outside the prison system the prisoner could hope for was whatever the Continental Congress might be able to provide or that which might be donated to the ships by concerned groups of private citizens. Naval prisoners were a tattered and mangy-looking lot. The summer months presented a minimum of difficulty to men lacking clothing and blankets, but the prisoners viewed the onset of winter with a feeling of something akin to terror. Winter was hard enough for a well-clad man to survive, but without decent clothing and bedding the chance of survival was greatly lessened.

Another of the difficulties the prisoners had to face was the food they were issued. The amount and the quality of the rations provided the men aboard the floating prisons was subject to considerable criticism throughout the war. Both the amount and the quality of the provisions doled out to the captives was suspect, and understandably the men who were imprisoned aboard the vessels were dissatisfied with their fare. Like the captive army personnel who received two-thirds the allowance of the British soldier, American seamen aboard the prison vessels drew two-thirds the allotment of the British seamen.[19] The weekly rations of the eighteenth century British seamen were not ample,[20] and to place men on two-thirds such a diet seemed severe to the captives. The British sailor had the opportunity to supplement his diet while ashore, whereas the prisoner had little opportunity to forage for himself. The British Navy's viewpoint was that prisoners of war needed less food than did a man on active duty, and it felt justified, as did the army, in issuing a fraction of the normal rations ordinarily provided to their personnel. As a result, American prisoners on the ships were poorly fed. American protests over the provisions alloted to American naval prisoners were frequent and vigorous. Eventually, the protests did bear some fruit. By 1781, the amount of food issued to the naval captives was increased to a point where the weekly rations slightly exceeded those alloted to British seamen. The provisions at this point amount to four pounds of bread or biscuit, two and one-half pounds of beef, one and one-half pounds of pork, eight ounces of butter, two pints of oatmeal, and one and one-sixth pints of peas per week.[21]

On paper, at least, the prisoners' food situation gradually improved during the war, but even so there are obvious shortcomings in their diet. The most glaring deficiencies were the lack of fresh vegetables and fruits, when in season, and dairy products of all sorts except for butter. Naturally there were many cases where the standard rations were not issued, and if the items were forthcoming, they were not always provided in the exact amounts expected by the prisoners. And of course the rations might be provided in the exact amount, but the quality might be so poor that they were inedible or of little nutritional value. In any event, the weekly menu was most monotonous, and no matter how hungry a man might be, it was often difficult for him to accept the food. Malnutrition and excessive loss of weight was endemic among the prisoners. Technically the British discharged their responsibility regarding the food for the captives most of the time, but the results left much to be desired.

The means of preparing the meager rations was unappetizing at the best. The inmates were divided into six-man messes, and each morning at nine o'clock one of the men who served as the steward received the daily ration for his mess. The steward then took the food to the boiler which was used to cook the food. The boiler was a huge vat, usually made of copper, which contained three hogsheads of water. The vat was divided into two parts. On one side there was fresh water to boil peas and oatmeal, and on the other side there was salt water to boil the meat. The food was placed in the boiler and cooked under the supervision of the cook who maintained order around the vat and who made certain that each mess steward withdrew only his allotment when the food was finished. When the mess steward first placed his food in the vat, he suspended a tally string over the side of the boiler to identify his rations. When the cook rang the bell, the steward was allowed to remove his food and to take it to his messmates. The boiler was never very clean, and the water used to prepare the meat was normally drawn from alongside the ship — the same area where the tubs from below were also emptied each day. The food was nearly repulsive when it was prepared. Some of the messes were able to accumulate their own cooking utensils and gained permission to prepare their food without using the common boiler. Stewards from these more fortunate messes gathered around the boiler with their kettles, pots, and pans and cooked their food over little fires they were permitted to build. Either way, the results of the stewards' efforts rarely received the unqualified approval of their messmates.[22] All of the conditions under which the food was prepared reflected, to a very large degree, the personality of the cook who supervised the whole process. A particularly authoritarian soul might make life much more unpleasant for the captives, whereas a gentler man could make the conditions a bit more tolerable.

The prisoners were allowed to purchase food from outside sources if they had the money to pay for it. Captain Thomas Dring, for example, was a captive aboard the *Jersey*, and he wrote of a corpulent old woman named Dame Grant who came alongside the vessel in a small boat every other day to sell such items as bread, fruit, tea, sugar, tobacco, needles, thread, and other goods to the men.[23] Apparently, the practice of permitting the prisoners to buy food and other items from sources outside the prison ships was widespread for the fortunate few who had the cash to do so.[24]

The daily routine of the prisoners was a monotonous one. Most of the time the captives whiled away the hours in eating, sleeping, quarreling, and waiting hopefully for a prisoner exchange. There were, however, duties which the prisoners could perform which helped to alter the routine somewhat. Volunteers from among the inmates were used to handle some of the daily chores. Normally, there was no shortage of men willing to work. Work helped to pass the time, and some of the chores got the labor parties off the ship for a brief time. The *Jersey*, for example, required seven hundred gallons of fresh water a day.[25] Each day a water party, composed of armed guards and prisoners, went ashore to get the water.[26] Service on the water detail was eagerly sought by the prisoners, since it afforded them the opportunity to enjoy a respite from the cramped and dismal conditions in the ship. The labor was strenuous, but the effort seemed to be worth the relative freedom it offered. Prisoners were often required to man the ship's pumps to keep the vessel from sinking.[27] This detail was not very popular. Periodically, a work party was chosen which was given buckets, brushes, and vinegar to scrub and cleanse the decks and bulkheads.[28] Work parties were also used to help hoist fuel and rations aboard, to care for the ill, and to perform myriad other duties. One of the reasons, aside from simply dispelling the boredom, that the work parties were popular among the captives was that a member of the detail drew a full ration of food for his work and a bonus of one-half pint of rum.[29] The food incentive was important, but the chance to vary the daily routine was equally as responsible for the willingness of the prisoners to work.

The most melancholy duty came in the morning when the prisoners were ordered to turn out their dead.[30] Deaths among captives were common. A burial detail, formed from among the prisoners, went ashore under an armed guard to bury the deceased.[31] This task was not very popular among the prisoners, but the burial party was usually quickly recruited from among the deceased man's friends or shipmates.

Probably the single greatest fear common to all of the captives was the rampant diseases they were exposed to on a daily basis. The crowded unsanitary conditions and the inadequate diet combined to produce a multitude of health problems for the inmates of the floating hulks. Two of the commonest ailments suffered by the captives, which were induced by the filth, unbalanced diet, and bad water, were scurvy and dysentery. Scurvy and dysentery were so common among the prisoners that it was virtually normal to be afflicted with one or both. In addition, the men lived in constant fear of such diseases as yellow fever and smallpox.[32] Pneumonia and influenza were also common among the captives and took a heavy toll of lives as well. In fact, the medical situation aboard one of the prison ships defies description. Any man who had been a prisoner for any length of time was usually in very poor health. It was virtually impossible for a captive, no matter how strong his constitution, to avoid the sickness that marked a prison ship.

The medical program established to tend to the needs of the men on the prison ships was, to say the least, a slipshod one. What passed for a medical program was most inadequate, and it dealt only with those who fell ill. No real effort was made to try to prevent the outbreak of disease. Admittedly, the era of preventive medicine had not yet arrived in the eighteenth century, but such measures as inoculation against smallpox would have saved many lives. Ordinarily, a prison ship was visited daily by a British physician if the weather was good. The doctor gave a casual inspection to the conditions of the ship and then turned his attention to the men who had answered the sick call.[33] The seriously ill were transferred to a hospital ship to isolate them from the healthier prisoners and to receive a little more efficient care.[34] The whole thrust of the medical care provided for the prisoners was to deal with a crisis once it arose and really to do little to try to prevent the epidemics which plagued the captives. The care the men received was usually a matter of much too little attention much too late. The death rate of the captives aboard the hospital ships was high. Occasionally, captured American doctors were lodged in one of the prison hulks, but there was little they could accomplish in view of the shortage of medical supplies, the unsanitary conditions, and the poor health of most of the men.[35] As a rule, the American physicians were soon paroled and moved elsewhere to await exchange. They were, consequently, able to do little for their countrymen.[36] To reiterate, the medical status of the prisoners was simply wretched. While the captives endured nearly impossible circumstances, it should be pointed out at this juncture, however, that the British faced a difficult task in trying to provide a semblance of medical care. Throughout the war the British never had the manpower or the supplies to deal effectively with the needs of the captives aboard the floating prisons. Most of the suffering of the captives arose not from premeditated cruelty on the part of the British, but rather from the breakdown of the apparatus which was supposed to cope with the needs of the prisoners of war. Nevertheless, the medical care was inadequate, and the responsibility for its shortcomings was Great Britain's.

Authority over captured seamen held prisoner in America rested in the hands of the Commander in Chief of British forces in America. As was the case with all American army personnel, the Commander in Chief was responsible for the care and exchange of captured seamen. The Commander in Chief had very little time to devote to the day-to-day matters of prison administration and prisoner care. Consequently, authority was delegated to someone else. The standard practice was for the Commander in Chief to delegate authority over captured American seamen to the commanding naval officer located at New York City, who in turn charged one of the junior officers on his staff to watch over the naval prison system. Because of frequent changes in command or lengthy absences of officers on sea duty, the number of people involved in the care of American seamen is truly astonishing. One man, however, was a part of the program to care for American captives held by the Royal Navy throughout the entire war. David Sproat was appointed Commissary General of Naval Prisoners and served at the post until the British withdrew from New York City in 1782.[37]

David Sproat was an American Loyalist who prior to the war had been a merchant in Philadelphia. He had joined the British in New York City after it was occupied in 1776.[38] A combination of his political connections and a recognition of his administrative skills secured his appointment as Commissary General of Naval Prisoners from General William Howe. The Commissary General operated under general regulations which were issued to him from time to time by the commanding naval officer in New

York City.[39] Sproat's responsibilities were many, as he was charged with the primary duty of seeing to the basic needs of the captured American seamen. Such matters as providing food, fuel, clothing, medical care, and other necessaries consumed most of his time and effort. Additionally, however, Sproat also managed the details concerning exchanges of naval prisoners. He carried on a lively correspondence with American authorities, answering letters of inquiry and protest about the conditions and treatment of the captives under his jurisdiction. While Sproat was well known and widely disliked by the rebels, he was an efficient and honest man who handled his duties as best he could under the difficult circumstances he faced. American prisoners did suffer under his administration. There is no argument which can prove otherwise, but the suffering was not due to an unconcerned Commissary General. Sproat did try to make conditions for the captives better, but he met with constant frustration and ultimately failed to alleviate their misery. Consequently, later generations looked back upon Sproat as some sort of unfeeling monster who personally was the author of the whole tragic episode of the prison ships. That is an unfair assessment of his work and efforts.

American naval personnel were imprisoned in a great many places outside the thirteen rebellious colonies. New York City, as the first part of this chapter indicates, was the primary site for detaining American seamen, but the circumstances of the naval war often dictated that other prisons in other geographical areas also be used. The great majority of American sailors captured by the British were from privateers. The American Continental Navy was never very large, nor was it very successful in operations against Great Britain. Privateering, on the other hand, flourished during the war, and the raiders stalked the main traffic lanes in the Atlantic, the English Channel, all around Great Britain, the Caribbean, and the Gulf of Mexico.

A privateer usually was a lightly armed vessel whose main asset was its speed. These ships were designed to seize enemy merchant vessels and to create havoc in Great Britain's maritime economy. When a privateer seized an enemy ship, the crew and owner of the raider shared in the proceeds from the sale of the captured ship and its cargo, which meant that privateering could be very profitable for all concerned. Privateering was, however, a risky occupation. If the raider encountered a British warship it could not outrun, or if it could not make a friendly port, the privateer was finished. Rarely was there a privateer fitted out which was any match for a British man-of-war. Naturally, many American privateers did suffer the misfortune of encountering a man-of-war and being forced to surrender. During the war hundreds of men were captured by the Royal Navy aboard the privateers. From the earliest days of the war, the prisons bulged with the captured seamen as they sat out the war hoping for a prisoner exchange, planning an escape, or just waiting for the conflict to end and to have their freedom restored.

Privateers often ranged thousands of miles in search of their prey. Because of their far-flung activities the crews of these vessels were scattered all over the Atlantic and adjoining waters when they became prisoners. Obviously, the Royal Navy could not waste time and ships transporting American captives from abroad to New York City every time a handful of men were captured. So, in addition to the naval prison system at New York City, several locations were employed to handle the flow of captured American sailors.

Throughout the war there were two main points where the naval prisoners were concentrated. One, of course, was the prison fleet at New York City, and the other was in Great Britain. Two prisons, Mill Prison and Forton Prison, were employed as permanent detention centers in Great Britain.[40] Sooner or later, unless they escaped or they were exchanged, naval prisoners captured outside American waters ended their journey in one of these two centers. Literally dozens of places saw temporary duty as prisons for the Americans until they could be sent off to New York or to Great Britain. A bewildering array of names arises when sites of temporary prisons are listed.

Contingents of American seamen were detained in several temporary prisons in the western hemisphere. As mentioned earlier, the prison ships named the *Torbay* and *Pack Horse* were employed at Charleston, South Carolina, to hold naval prisoners taken there. Other sites were used too. Occasionally, men from privateers seized in the northern Atlantic were brought to Halifax, Nova Scotia, and placed in the Old Jail prior to their being sent to New York or to Great Britain.[41] The island of Barbados, in the West Indies, was often used as a collection point for men taken in the Caribbean area by the Royal Navy. In 1782, for example, 254 Americans were being held on Barbados[42] awaiting transportation to New York, and more prisoners were on their way to the island at that point.[43] The island of St. Lucia, where the prison ship *Peter* was located, also was employed as a temporary site to detain naval prisoners.[44] A few American seamen spent some time in the Leeward Islands as prisoners prior to being sent on to New York.[45] The use of Barbados, St. Lucia, and the Leeward Islands was only an expedient for the Royal Navy. The islands were drop points for men-of-war to shed their prisoners. Then the captives were to be moved on to a permanent prison where they could be offered for exchange — usually New York City.

There were a number of temporary prisons outside the western hemisphere too. American captives could be found almost any place a British warship might be on duty. Warships regularly carried the men they captured with them, sometimes for weeks, until they could reach a port where they might turn them over to some government agency. The prisoners were then sent on to England for disposition in permanent quarters. Outside the western hemisphere Americans were detained in such places as Senegal in Africa, Portugal, and the island of Guernsey before being transported to England.[46] Ultimately, if they did not escape or if they were not exchanged, the prisoners captured in African or European waters ended their journey in Mill Prison near Plymouth, England, or in Forton Prison near Portsmouth, England.[47] Mill and Forton prisons were designated as sites to hold captured American seamen in 1777.[48] So, while Americans could be found almost anywhere, the two prisons at Portsmouth and Plymouth were the focal points of detention of men captured outside American waters.

Forton and Mill prisons became notorious in America before the war finally ended. Forton prison was originally constructed to serve as a hospital to care for sick and wounded seamen of the British Navy. Then in 1777 it was converted into a prison to detain captured American seamen.[49] At the time that Forton was designated a prison, it was composed of two large, spacious buildings which housed the captives. Adjacent to the compound there was an area three-quarters of an acre in size which was used as an exercise field for the inmates. The exercise area was guarded by armed sentries, but, even so, the men were permitted to roam the small field and to enjoy the open air and sunshine. On the field there was a small open-sided shed in which the men could sit and while away the hours with conversation and card games.[50] The environment at Forton, under the circumstances, was agreeable, and the inmates were given more freedom than in most other British prisons. Mill prison was a little larger than Forton. Four large buildings of about three thousand square feet each composed the quarters of the prisoners.[51] The men at Mill Prison did not enjoy the same amount of freedom as those at Forton, but the prison was reasonably clean, spacious, and well maintained. Certainly the men at both prisons were much better off than the sailors held in the prison ships at New York.

In fact, many more precautions were taken to care for the health and well-being of the men in Forton and Mill than anywhere else Americans were detained. When a prisoner arrived at one of these prisons he was issued a hammock, a straw mattress, a blanket, and a pillow and assigned to his quarters.[52] The men lived in large rooms of several hundred square feet in size in what amounted to a dormitory. The hammocks were slung from the walls each evening and taken down in the morning to create more space for the men. While the sleeping arrangements were not ideal, they probably were not a great deal worse than they had been on the ships the men had been taken from. Clothing was also issued to the men periodically; the men imprisoned in the navy prisons in New York would have been amazed over this fact. The annual clothing ration issued to the men in Mill and Forton amounted to a jacket, a waistcoat, a pair of breeches, shoes and a cap, two shirts, and two pairs of stockings.[53] The clothing allotment was not extravagant by any means, but it was, with careful use, adequate. The important point to stress, however, is that the men held in England did receive more consideration from their captors than did those in America.

Each day washing troughs, soap, and water were made available to the inmates so they could bathe and wash their clothing. The bathing and washing facilities were heavily taxed by the numbers of the men using them, but, again, the prison officials did make an effort to see to the hygenic needs of the men.[54] The bedding and clothing issues were not what the prisoners wanted in every case; but these men were much more fortunate than most other captives.

The food at Mill and Forton prisons was the subject of some controversy. Prisoners were rarely satisfied with amount and the quality of the food doled out daily by the commissary. Each day, usually at noon, the daily portion of food was distributed and each man was allowed to take his provisions to a separate cookhouse to prepare them.[55] On a weekly basis the total amount of rations given to a prisoner was supposed to amount to seven pounds of bread, four and one-half pounds of meat, two pints of peas or greens, and either four ounces of butter or six ounces of cheese, seven quarts of beer, and two and one-third ounces of salt.[56] The food rations were, apparently, faithfully distributed, but they were only adequate in amount. About all a prisoner could rely upon was one fairly substantial meal per day with such a portion of food being alloted to him, and the captives were quick to point this out to their jailors and to criticize the amount. While the quantity of the food was not overwhelming, it also became a monotonous diet. Occasionally, the quality of the rations was none too good either, but, on the whole, the food was tolerable.

Controversy over the food allotment, excepting the ongoing quarrel over the quantity of the rations, centered around bread. The American captives eventually learned that the French and Spanish prisoners of war received ten and one-half pounds of bread per week, while they got only seven pounds per week. The Americans complained regularly about the difference and asked that they also receive the ten and one-half pound ration of bread. The reason for the difference, the Americans were told, was that since 1745 rebels had been issued seven pounds of bread a week, and that they should expect no more. Furthermore, they were informed that Great Britain alloted ten and one-half pounds of bread a week to prisoners of war, and that this fact explained why the French and Spanish received more bread than the Americans. Finally, however, in 1782 the Government increased the weekly bread allotment to ten and one-half pounds a week for the Americans.[57] Except for the difference in the bread, the provisions issued to the Americans and the foreign captives were the same.

Prisoners were allowed to supplement their diet by purchasing whatever food they could afford. Every day from ten to three o'clock an open market was held at the prison gates where the inmates could buy all sorts of items. Local farmers and merchants came to the prison and sold food, clothing, and other necessaries of life to the men. The inmates could not purchase alcoholic beverages, but almost anything else was permitted to enter the prison via the open market.[58] Mostly the prisoners bought food to augment their rations, extra clothing, and such items as books, paper, pens, and ink to help to pass the hours away by writing, studying, and keeping diaries. The only obstacle was the need for money to buy the supplies. The prisoners resorted to a number of means to accumulate cash. Many of the prisoners began to manufacture such things as ladles, spoons, boxes, chairs, and tables to be sold for cash or to be bartered at the open market.[59] Occasionally, groups of prisoners secured permission to place a charity box outside the prison, and whatever sums of money were placed in it were divided among the group.[60] Normally the men were permitted to solicit gifts from the people who visited the prison or to ask for donations from concerned local residents.[61] Additionally, any gift of money from any person, even if it came from American sources, was allowed to reach the prisoners.[62]

Many friends and relatives of the captives managed to get small sums of money to them irregularly. When the money arrived the prison officials quickly turned it over to the man it was supposed to reach. On this point, the honesty of the prison officials and staff seems to have been faultless. Some of the more concerned citizens of Great Britain also raised money by subscription to assist the prisoners and to reduce their financial distress. Most informed persons were aware of the men and of their need for money to purchase extra food and a few luxuries; so in 1777, for example, a group of prominent London people raised £800 and donated it to the prisoners for division among themselves.[63] The money came with no strings attached. The prisoners were to be allowed to divide it among themselves, and the manner in which each man spent the funds he received was his own business. Several of these subscriptions were raised during the war. They were noble gestures on the part of a group of humanitarian people, but, unfortunately, the gestures fell far short of the needs of the men. So while there were several ways that cash might reach the prisoners, they always had need of more than they could manage to acquire. It should be stressed, however, that although the prisoners suffered from a chronic shortage of funds, the British government, the prison officials, and the prison staff did not attempt to deny them any legitimate access to earning money, to receiving gifts or donations of money, or simply to bartering for what items they wished to acquire. The attitude toward the prisoners on this issue was essentially a permissive one which the captives must have noticed and appreciated.

Medical care was also provided for the captives, although it was not as complete as the men may have desired. At Mill and Forton prisons the inmates received more medical attention, on a regular basis, than Americans held captive anywhere else during the Revolution. All sorts of regulations were enforced to protect their health. Such procedures as providing soap and water regularly, fumigation of bedding and clothing, and burning the bedding and clothing which were suspected of being infected were rigorously observed.

Opportunities for fresh air, sunshine, and exercise were routinely open to the prisoners, and they were forcefully encouraged to try to control vermin. New prisoners were carefully inspected upon their arrival at the prison and automatically quarantined if they were suspected of carrying an infectious disease. The inmates already in the prison were also periodically examined, and if one appeared to be falling ill he was removed to the hospital to isolate him from the other prisoners. As a result, a fairly effective program of preventive medicine, by eighteenth century standards, was established which was reasonably effective in protecting the men from excessive exposure to hardship. Both prisons had small, adequately staffed hospitals to tend to the needs of their inmates.[64]

Surgeons from the Royal Navy were assigned duty in the hospitals, where they fulfilled their appointments faithfully. Prisoners were called upon to volunteer to work in the hospitals, to nurse patients, to scrub floors, and to perform many other tasks associated with keeping the wards clean and functioning smoothly. With the volunteer help, the hospital staff managed to conduct an acceptable medical program for the men. Due in large measure to the hospitals and the health regulations, the death rate in Mill and Forton prisons was low in comparison with other prisons where American naval personnel were detained.[65] The prisoners in Mill and Forton prisons were never fully aware of their advantages, but they were much better off than other of their countrymen who were captured during the American Revolution.

The treatment the prisoners received, aside from food, clothing, and medical care, was also much discussed during the war. Wars nearly always produce chilling accounts of brutal mistreatment of captives, but the men in Mill and Forton were very fortunate in this regard. Actual physical mistreatment of the prisoners by their guards was quite uncommon.[66] Physical blows were sometimes struck by the guards when they were angered or frustrated. The minor outbreaks of violence by the guards were rare, and then they were nearly always provoked by the inmates. Naturally, the guards regularly abused the captives verbally, and little could be done about that. The inmates also delivered a flood of verbal abuse upon their guards in retaliation, and not much harm was done in this kind of exchange.

A steady stream of criticism and demands for investigation of the prisons in England was maintained by prominent American leaders.[67] Actually, there really was not much to investigate. The American demands for investigation were more often made to try to raise the morale of the men in the prisons or for their propaganda value in the colonies than for any other reason. There were many points on which the British were vulnerable, true enough, but, on balance, the men were not treated too badly, and the American authorities knew it.

Two forms of punishment were officially sanctioned in Mill and Forton prisons. One was solitary confinement on half rations in what the prisoners usually called the "black hole."[68] The other was to place the names of unruly prisoners at the bottom of the exchange list.[69] When a captive entered prison his name was placed at the bottom of a list of men eligible for exchange. As the weeks passed by, and as partial exchanges of captives were made, his name would rise on the list, bringing him closer to the day he might be exchanged. The hope for exchange was a powerful inducement to render men more cooperative. If a prisoner became especially obstreperous or dangerous he was restrained with chains, but the incidents of men being placed in irons were relatively few in number.

Most of the severe punishment, especially solitary confinement, was meted out to prisoners who tried to escape. Literally scores of men made bids for freedom by trying to escape. Every imaginable means of escape was used by the men, but two means proved to be the most popular and productive. The easiest way to escape, if one had enough money, was to bribe one of the guards and simply, with his help, slip out of the prison.[70]

It was risky, of course, because the guard might take the bribe and then report it to the prison authorities, and the American would end up in the "black hole." Or a guard might accept the money and then fail to live up to his part of the bargain, leaving the American out a considerable sum of precious money. So it had its elements of chance, but if the inmate chose his contact among the guards wisely, bribery was the safest and quickest way of fleeing the prison. The other popular technique of escape was to tunnel out of the prison.

Tunneling was very popular among the captives even though it was dangerous and time consuming.[71] The tunnels did not have to be very long, but the logistics were complicated, and the problems of such an endeavor were difficult to overcome. In addition to these methods, prisoners also slipped down drains and sewers, scaled walls, overpowered guards, and so forth, in efforts to escape. The prison guards constantly searched for tunnels, held surprise roll calls, and employed every conceivable tactic to try to frustrate escape plots. To a discouraging degree, the prison staff proved successful in uncovering plots before they were consummated, but many men still escaped.

When prisoners escaped they proceeded toward the English Channel to try to get to France or the Netherlands. Surprisingly, some captives succeeded in their efforts.[72] Escape in a country where the prisoners shared the same language and racial characteristics would at first appear easy, but that was not the case at all. The prisoner's clothing, or lack of clothing, physical appearance, and even his speech betrayed him. Additionally, there was a £5 bounty paid to English citizens for assistance in recovering escaped rebels which meant that in vicinities around the prisons the local inhabitants kept a wary and enterprising eye on all strangers.[73] The risks in trying to escape and the penalties for failing were obvious, but they did little to deter the captives.[74]

Authority over the captured American seamen in Great Britain was shared by several government agencies. The status of the prisoners was a unique one in that they were not classified as prisoners of war until 1782, and, as a result, they were dealt with as a domestic problem rather than as one involving foreign personnel. Day-to-day authority over the Americans was the prerogative of the Royal Navy, but the policy regarding the captives was evolved under the direction of the Secretary of State for the Northern Department, the Lords Commissioners of the Admiralty, and one of the Lords Commissioners of the Admiralty's subordinate boards, the Commissioners for Sick and Hurt Seamen and the Exchange of Prisoners.[75] All three groups played a role in determining the care and exchange of American seamen taken prisoner by the Royal Navy.

Temporary wartime commissions for sick and hurt seamen and the exchange of prisoners had existed since 1689,[76] but by the time of the American Revolution a permanent commission had been established. The commission was composed of one medical man and several civilians who fulfilled a variety of responsibilities, but it was they who directly superintended the care the Americans received while they were captives in Great Britain.[77] The Commissioners for Sick and Hurt Seamen and the Exchange of Prisoners were concerned with establishing directives as to the daily care and living conditions of the captives. This commission was heavily influenced by the views of the Lords Commissioners of the Admiralty since it was a subordinate board to the admiralty. Nevertheless, it was a very active and somewhat independent body which worked vigorously to control the environment Americans endured while in British prisons.

Both the Secretary of State for the Southern Department and the Secretary of State for the Northern Department were, from time to time, involved in the prisoner of war issue when diplomatic questions arose. In addition to the matter of diplomatic involvement, the Secretary of State for the Northern Department exercised considerable authority over the American seamen. He authorized exchanges, dealt with security matters, issued paroles and pardons, and handled most of the legal matters concerning the captives held in Great Britain.[78] Occasionally, the Secretary of State for the Southern Department became involved in the fate of American captives, but normally his contact with the issue of American captives was slight. It was really the Secretary of State for the Northern Department and the Commissioners for Sick and Hurt Seamen and the Exchange of Prisoners who, in conjunction with the Royal Navy, handled the bulk of matters affecting captured American seamen. All in all, considering the different departments involved, the administration of the issues regarding the American captives in Great Britain was executed smoothly and efficiently even though it sometimes bewildered and frustrated Americans who attempted to comprehend the system.

Very few statistics are available concerning the numbers of American seamen held captive by the British. As mentioned before, the overwhelming majority of the captured sailors came from the privateers which roamed the major shipping lanes of the tributory waters of the Atlantic and the Atlantic itself in search of enemy merchant vessels to prey upon. The ubiquitous American raiders took a heavy toll of British ships, and the navy labored diligently to drive them from the seas to safeguard Great Britain's commerce. As a result of the far flung activity of the privateers and the concerted effort of the Royal Navy to curtail their depredations upon England's shipping, many American vessels were apprehended in an amazing variety of locations in the western hemisphere and in the coastal waters of western Europe. Consequently, American crews from privateers were scattered among a great many different prisons in a number of different places.

Two major problems arise in trying to assess the total of Americans who were destined to end their naval activities in a British prison. The first one is that the scattered nature of the prisons did not promote any central record keeping on the part of the British authorities. As a rule, the various prisons did not coordinate their administration of captives and compile prisoner lists for exchange among themselves. Each prison seemed to act independently of the others, and little information was passed back and forth among the compounds. As a result, accurate prison records about the names and other vital statistics of captives were difficult to obtain at the time of the Revolution — a circumstance which the passage of two hundred years has not improved for the modern day researcher. The second complication which emerges in trying to count the numbers of the captives is that the Royal Navy did not trouble itself, as did the army, to keep accurate tabulations of its captives. About all one can do, as a result, is to provide some general figures which are unsatisfactory at best but can give some insight into the numbers of captives detained by the British Navy.

American seamen were seized in privateering vessels from the very beginning of the war, but it was not until 1777 that the Royal Navy began to take great numbers of captives. By the end of 1777, at least 429 men were under detention in Great Britain, and perhaps as many as two thousand seamen were in prisons in North America.[79] So, at the end of 1777, approximately 2,500 despairing American seamen awaited exchange. During 1778 and 1779, many more American privateers were captured by the British, and the naval prisons bulged with captives. There was a dramatic rise in the numbers of Americans incarcerated in Great Britain. For example, *The Annual Register* for 1778 asserted that 942 seamen were imprisoned in England and Ireland,[80] and, in 1779, it claimed that 2,200 men resided in the various prisons of Great Britain as a result of being captured by the Royal Navy.[81] The figure of 2,200 American seamen jailed in Great Britain alone was the largest total for that phase of the war. From 1778 to the end of the war, the total of Americans in prison in the British Isles usually hovered around one thousand except for the peak point which was reached in 1779. The men held in captivity in England and Ireland were, however, only one-half of the picture, as a great many men also languished in prisons elsewhere.

Outside of Great Britain, most of the captured American naval personnel were located in the New York City area. The records concerning captives held at New York City are discouragingly few prior to 1779. In the early years of the war, sizeable numbers of men were taken in privateers in American coastal waters and delivered to the prison ships at New York City. The captives were placed aboard the floating hulks and offered for exchange. Few exchanges were consummated in the first two years of the war, however, due largely to the fact that not many British naval personnel had fallen into American hands. The result was, of course, that by 1779 the British faced a serious problem of controlling and caring for so many men. Finally the situation became so acute that on October 13, 1779, David Sproat was appointed to the position of Commissary General of Naval Prisoners.[82]

Sproat was directed to exchange or, as necessary, parole naval prisoners to reduce the captive population of the burdened prisons, and he attacked the problem with considerable vigor. Unfortunately, Sproat was not much of a record keeper, but he did produce the first useful information one can employ. In the first year of his tenure of office, Sproat arranged to exchange three thousand American seamen.[83] On October 12, 1780, Sproat, who had already exchanged three thousand, reported that a total of 1,200 remained aboard the prison ships.[84] The evidence indicates, therefore, that in late 1779 and in early 1780 the greatest number of American seamen were under detention in Great Britain and America. During this period, Sproat had exercised authority over the fate of approximately 4,200 men, and the Continental Congress estimated at this same period that about 1,062 Americans were imprisoned in Great Britain.[85] Using these estimates, a figure of approximately 5,300 naval captives would probably represent the highest total detained by the British at one time.

After early 1780 the number of men jailed in the British naval prisons declined steadily. Occasionally there was some fluctuation upward during brief periods, but the overall trend was always for the number of naval prisoners to diminish after 1780. By the end of 1781, for example, Benjamin Franklin estimated that eight hundred Americans were lodged in prisons in Great Britain, and David Sproat reported that he had about five hundred seamen under his care at New York City.[86] A total of not many more than 1,300 men would represent a fairly accurate account of the Americans sitting out the war in naval prisons. Compared with the number of captives detained by Great Britain in late 1779 and in early 1780, the decline was substantial. Then in the early part of 1782, the sum of Americans held prisoners of war by the Royal Navy increased slightly. In March of 1782, Franklin estimated that a total of one thousand Americans were detained in the British Isles,[87] and, at New York City, David Sproat claimed to have seven hundred seamen under his care.[88] Later in 1782 the total of captive American seamen slightly exceeded two thousand, but the flow of fresh prisoners never approached the record pace of 1779 and 1780.[89]

As peace was concluded in 1783, the rate of repatriation was accelerated and finally completed by mid-1783.[90] An actual count of the number of men captured and imprisoned by the Royal Navy simply can not be compiled. A host of problems arises when trying to develop a census of the captives. As mentioned before, the eighteenth century did not exhibit the modern day penchant for precise record keeping, and what few documents survived are incomplete. The material only hints at answers and does little to provide solid evidence upon which reliable totals may be computed. An educated guess concerning the absolute number of men captured by the British Navy would be not more than eight thousand seamen throughout the entire war.

FOOTNOTES

[1] Dandridge, *American Prisoners*, 91. Armbruster, *Prison Ships*, 15. George Washington to Richard, Lord Howe, January 12, 1777, Fitzpatrick, *Writings of Washington*, VII, 3-5.

[2] Dandridge, *American Prisoners*, 493. Albert G. Greene, ed., *Recollections of the Jersey Prison-Ship; Taken and Prepared for Publication from the Original Manuscript of the Late Captain Thomas Dring of Providence, R. I.* (Providence, 1829), XIII, 19. Cited hereafter as Greene, *Recollections*. Onderdonck, *Revolutionary Incidents*, 235-36.

[3] Greene, *Recollections*, 22, 166-67. Philip Freneau, "Some Account of the Capture of the Ship Aurora," Philip Freneau Collections, Rutgers University Library, New Brunswick, New Jersey, 7. Cited hereafter as Freneau, "Some Account." Moore, *Diary*, II, 219-20. Onderdonck, *Revolutionary Incidents*, 230. Dandridge, *American Prisoners*, 496.

[4] Thomas Andros, *The Old Jersey Captive: A Narrative of the Captivity of Thomas Andros (now Pastor of the Church in Berkley) on board the Old Jersey Prison Ship at New York, 1781* (Boston, 1833), 8. Cited hereafter as Andros, *Jersey*.

[5] Bushnell, *Narrative of Blatchford*, 117. Force, *American Archives*, III, 519, 907, 1138. Dandridge, *American Prisoners*, 132, 493, 496. Onderdonck, *Revolutionary Incidents*, 230, 231-32, 244. James Lennox Banks, *David Sproat and Naval Prisoners in the War of the Revolution* (New York, 1909), 101. Cited hereafter as Banks, *Sproat*. Freneau, "Some

Account," 7. Moore, *Diary*, II, 219-20. David L. Sterling, "American Prisoners of War in New York: A Report by Elias Boudinot," *William and Mary Quarterly*, Third Series, XII (1956), 391.

⁶Greene, *Recollections*, 21, 73. Onderdonck, *Revolutionary Incidents*, 244. Dandridge, *American Prisoners*, 319. Charles E. West, "Prison Ships in the American Revolution," *Journal of American History*, V (1911), 122.

⁷JCC, XX, 621. PCC, Roll 177, Item 158, 509, 513-14. R. W. Gibbes, *Documentary History of the American Revolution Consisting of Letters and Papers Relating to the Contest for Liberty, Chiefly in South Carolina, In 1781 and 1782* (Columbia, South Carolina, 1853), 76. Cited hereafter as Gibbes, *Documentary History*.

⁸George, Lord Rodney, *Letter-Books and Order-Book of George, Lord Rodney Admiral of the White Squadron, 1780-1782* (New York, 1932), II, 523-24, 630, 592. Cited hereafter Rodney, *Letter-Book*.

⁹Andros, *Jersey*, 8. Onderdonck, *Revolutionary Incidents*, 235-36.

¹⁰Greene, *Recollections*, 30-31.

¹¹*Ibid.* Jack Coggins, *Ships and Seamen of the American Revolution* (Harrisburg, Pennsylvania, 1969), 79-81. Cited hereafter Coggins, *Ships and Seamen*.

¹²*Ibid.*

¹³Greene, *Recollections*, 88-89.

¹⁴*Ibid.*

¹⁵Andros, *Jersey*, 12. Andros was placed in the *Jersey*. At the time he went aboard the ship he reckoned the number of inmates at four hundred. He wrote, however, that the total soon reached an unbelievable twelve hundred. George Washington to The Officer Commanding the British Fleet at New York, January 28, 1781, Fitzpatrick, *Writings of Washington*, XXI, 134-44. Robert Magaw to Henry Clinton, November 30, 1777, Clinton Papers. Banks, *Sproat*, 34-36. Onderdonck, *Revolutionary Incidents*, 215-16.

¹⁶Derangement was common among the prisoners. Andros records that prisoners often became dangerous. He recalled hearing one night another prisoner call out "Take heed to yourselves. There is a man stalking through the ship with a knife in his hand." Andros, *Jersey*, 13.

¹⁷Greene, *Recollections*, 28.

¹⁸John Beatty to President of Congress, January 19, 1779, PCC, Roll 91, Item 78, 265-66. Beatty's description of the need of clothing and bedding among the prisoners is typical of dozens of such observations.

¹⁹Helen Jordan, ed., "Colonel Elias Boudinot in New York City, February 2, 1781," *The Pennsylvania Magazine of History and Biography*,

XXIV (1900), 460. This is the diary of Colonel Boudinot which records his views on the conditions of the captives while he was making an inspection trip to New York City. He was allowed to enter the city to see for himself that the American prisoners of war were not being treated badly.

[20] Enquiry on the treatment of Naval prisoners of war by the British officers, February 2, 1781, Banks, *Sproat*, 50-54. Dandridge, *American Prisoners*, 339-40. A full ration for a British seaman was three pounds of bread or biscuit, one pound of pork, two pounds of beef, one pint of oatmeal, one-half pint of peas, two ounces of butter, two ounces of suet and one and one-half pounds of flour per week.

[21] *Ibid.*

[22] Greene, *Recollections*, 39, 43, 98-99. Dandridge, *American Prisoners*, 339-340. Coggins, *Ships and Seamen*, 80-81.

[23] Greene, *Recollections*, 93-95.

[24] Bushnell, *Narrative of Blatchford*, 120-21. Dandridge, *American Prisoners*, 500.

[25] Andros, *Jersey*, 24-29. Greene, *Recollections*, 91.

[26] *Ibid.*

[27] Andros, *Jersey*, 9.

[28] *Ibid.*, 16.

[29] Greene, *Recollections*, 64-68.

[30] Extract of a letter from a man aboard the *Jersey*, August 10, 1781, Stiles, *Letters*, 31-32.

[31] *Ibid.*, 30. Greene, *Recollections*, 77-79.

[32] Andros, *Jersey*, 12-13. Greene, *Recollections*, 36-38. Freneau, "Some Account," 9-14. George Washington to Rear Admiral Robert Digby, June 25, 1782, Fitzpatrick, *Writings of Washington*, XXIV, 315-16.

[33] Greene, *Recollections*, 73. Banks, *Sproat*, 101.

[34] Armbruster, *Prison Ships*, 8, 18.

[35] Andros, *Jersey*, 15.

[36] *Ibid.*

[37] Sabine, *Sketches*, II, 234-35.

[38] *Ibid.*

[39] Rodney, *Letter-Book*, I, 34.

[40] One often finds Forton Prison referred to as "Fortune Prison." This is an error which apparently first appeared in the nineteeth century editions of diaries and memoirs of men held there. It is occasionally repeated today. See Charles H. Metzger, *Prisoner in the Revolution*, 48.

[41] Bushnell, *Narrative of Blatchford*, 10, 73n.

[42] James Cunningham to Rodney, March 3, 1782, Rodney, *Letter-Book*, I, 251.

[43] Rodney to Captain McLaurin, H.M.S. Triton, May 5, 1782, *ibid.*, II, 592.

[44] Rodney to Major General James Cunningham, Governor of Barbados, December 1, 1780, *ibid.*, I, 89-91. Rodney to Captain Cotton, H.M.S. Alarm, March 29, 1782, *ibid.*, II, 630.

[45] Captain John LaForey to Rodney, March 13, 1782, *ibid.*, I, 285-86.

[46] Franklin, Lee, and Adams to Lord North, June 4, 1778, L. H. Butterfield, ed., *Diary and Autobiography of John Adams* (Cambridge, Massachusetts, 1961), IV, 128, 236. Cited hereafter as Butterfield, *Diary of John Adams.*

[47] *Ibid.*, 138. William Cutler, ed., "Timothy Connor Journal," *The New England Historical and Genealogical Register*, XXXII, (1878), 186. Cited hereafter as Cutler, "Journal."

[48] *Gentlemen's Magazine*, XLVII, May, (1777), 194. Francis Abell, *Prisoners of War In Britain, 1756 to 1815* (Oxford, 1914), 214-34. John K. Alexander, "Forton Prison During The American Revolution: A Case Study of The British Prisoner of War Policy And The American Prisoner Response to That Policy," *The Essex Institute Historical Collections*, CIII (1967), 369. Cited hereafter as Alexander, "Forton Prison."

[49] Fanning, *Narrative*, 9. Olive Anderson, "Treatment Of Prisoners Of War," 66.

[50] Fanning, *Narrative*, 9-12, 16, 143.

[51] Cutler, "Journal," 186. William Hammond Bowden, ed., "Diary of William Widger of Marblehead, Kept at Mill Prison, England, 1781," *The Essex Institute Historical Proceedings,* LXXIII (1937), 313-16. Cited hereafter as Bowden, *Diary of Widger.*

[52] *Ibid.*, Rev. R. Livesey, ed., *The Prisoners of 1776; A Relic of the Revolution* (Boston, 1854), 90. Cited hereafter as Livesey, *Prisoners of 1776.* Fanning, *Narrative*, 16.

[53] Anderson, "Treatment of Prisoners of War," 73.

[54] Livesey, *Prisoners of 1776*, 98-99.

[55] *Ibid.*, 50-52. Anderson, "Treatment of Prisoners of War," 72.

[56] *Ibid. The Town and Country Magazine*, XLVI, September, (1781), 467. Cutler, "Journal," 186-87.

[57] Anderson, "Treatment of Prisoners of War," 72n. The Duke of Richmond was especially active in the fight to increase the bread allotment for the American captives.

[58] *Ibid.* Livesey, *Prisoners of 1776*, 52-53. Naturally such things as tools, potential weapons, and escape equipment were forbidden, but, other than these items, the prisons were very lenient about the inmates' right to buy goods from outside.

[59]Cutler, "Journal," 187. Bowden, *Diary of Widger*, 322-30.

[60]Livesey, *Prisoners of 1776*, 51-53.

[61]*Ibid.* On weekends the prisons were often visited by numbers of curious people who came to look at the captives. These visitors were usually good for a few contributions for the captives who were not too proud to ask for money.

[62]*Ibid.* William R. Cutter, ed., "A Yankee Privateersman in Prison in England, 1777-1779," *The New England Historical and Genealogical Register*, XXX (1876), 347. Cited hereafter Cutter, "Yankee Privateersman." For example, a Captain James Thompson, who had escaped from prison, sent twenty guineas from France to his shipmates. They got the money and divided it among themselves and bought food with it at the open market.

[63]Marquis de Noailles to Count de Vergennes, December 26, 1777, B. F. Stevens, ed., *Facsimiles of Manuscripts in European Archives Relating to America, 1773-1783* (London, 1889-1895), XX, Doc. 1803, 15-17. Cited hereafter as Stevens, *Facsimiles.* Among the contributors to this fund were Lord Shelburne, Lord Abingdon, and other prominent public officials.

[64]Anderson, "Treatment of Prisoners of War," 73.

[65]*Ibid.,* 75-76. Livesey, *Prisoners of 1776,* 109. Richard Livesey, ed., *A Relic of the Revolution* (Boston, 1847), 103. Cited hereafter Livesey, *Relic.*

[66]Fanning, *Narrative,* 12.

[67]American Commissioners to Committee of Correspondence, April 9, 1777, Stevens, *Facsimiles,* XIV, Doc. 1443, 14. Marquis de Noailles to Count de Vergennes, December 12, 1777, *ibid.,* XX, Doc. 1772, 15-16. John Jay to Thomas Johnson, November 8, 1777, *ibid.,* III, Doc. 295, 4. Franklin, Deane, and Lee to Lord North, December 12, 1777, *Gentlemen's Magazine,* XLVIII, January, (1778), 14-15.

[68]Fanning, *Narrative,* 13. Livesey, *Relic,* 105.

[69]Anderson, "Treatment of Prisoners of War," 74. Alexander, "Forton Prison," 370.

[70]Livesey, *Prisoners of 1776,* 51, 60, 78, 82, 126, 137-38, 152-53. Cutler, "Journal," 395. Cutter, "Yankee Privateersman," 166.

[71]Livesey, *Prisoners of 1776,* 100-115.

[72]Cutler, "Journal," 397. Diary of Abigail Adams, July 3, 1784, Butterfield, *Diary of John Adams,* III, 162.

[73]Anderson, "Treatment of Prisoners of War," 74.

[74]Charles Herbert was a prisoner in Mill prison where he recorded in his diary the escape of four men on July 12, 1777, three on July 25, 1777,

thirty-two by tunnel on August 5, 1777, one on October 5, 1777, one on October 6, 1777, five on January 31, 1778. Escapes were obviously common. Most of the men were caught and returned after being at large for several days to several weeks. Livesey, *Relic*, 57, 58, 60, 72, 100. It was estimated that 536 men escaped from Forton Prison between June 1777 and April 1782. Alexander, "Forton Prison," 382.

[75] Anderson, "Treatment of Prisoners of War," 64.

[76] J. Ehrman, *The Navy in the War of William III, 1686-1697* (Cambridge, 1953), 176.

[77] Anderson, "Treatment of Prisoners of War," 64n.

[78] *Ibid.*, 65n. The colonial secretary had authority over prisoners who had been captured in America and transported to Great Britain. After the first year or so of the war few Americans captured in America were brought to Britain.

[79] Livesey, *Prisoners of 1776*, 92. Banks, *Sproat*, 5. Cutler, *Journal*, 187, 307, 397.

[80] *The Annual Register*, 1778, XXI, 162. Alexander, "Forton Prison," 369.

[81] *The Annual Register, 1779*, XXII, 228.

[82] Banks, *Sproat*, 4.

[83] Rodney to Commissioners for Sick and Hurt Seamen, October 12, 1780, Rodney, *Letter-Books*, I, 34-35. According to Lord Rodney, only 1,400 naval personnel had returned to service through the exchanges. After Sproat began his term of office, the British exchanged seamen on account with the understanding that when new prisoners were taken the Americans would then make up the balance. Normally, the American authorities owed several hundred men to Sproat because of this rather generous policy.

[84] *Ibid.* Banks, *Sproat*, 125-26.

[85] PCC, Roll 97, Item 78, XIII, 151, 159. The reason for the decline was due to several exchanges, a few escapes, and a number of deaths among the prisoners of war in Great Britain.

[86] Franklin to Robert R. Livingston, March 4, 1781, Smyth, *Writings of Franklin*, VIII, 322-24. Banks, *Sproat*, 19. Bowden, *Diary of Widger*, 318.

[87] Franklin to Robert R. Livingston, March 4, 1781, Smyth, *Writings of Franklin*, VIII, 392.

[88] Banks, *Sproat*, 19.

[89] Franklin to John Jay, April 24, 1782, Henry P. Johnston, ed., *The Correspondence and Public Papers of John Jay* (New York, 1890-1893), II, 194. Cited hereafter as Johnston, *Correspondence of Jay*. Banks, *Sproat*, 19.

[90] Banks, *Sproat*, 19. Sproat reported on April 17, 1783, that all prisoners of war under his jurisdiction had been released. Burnett, *Letters*, VIII, 141n, 142, 160. JCC, XXIV, 140. George Washington to Secretary at War, July 1, 1783, Fitzpatrick, *Writings of Washington*, XXVII, 41.

chapter four

American Aid to American Captives

As the possibility of a war with Great Britain loomed larger in early 1776, the Continental Congress began to discuss the need of an agency to direct the affairs involving prisoners of war. On May 16, 1776, the members of Congress reached a tentative agreement and resolved that some sort of department ought to be created which could carry out the policies of Congress relevant to prisoners of war.[1] After nearly another month of intermittent debate, the Congress ordered, on June 12, 1776, that a Board of War and Ordnance be established.[2]

The Board of War and Ordnance consisted of five members of Congress elected to the agency by their fellow congressmen. Actually, the Board of War and Ordnance was required to perform many tasks, but for the purposes of this study only its duties regarding captives will be examined. Its function regarding captives was twofold. The Board of War and Ordnance was ordered to oversee the direction and care of British captives held by American forces, and also to lend whatever material support it could provide to Americans detained by the British. From the beginning, the Board of War and Ordnance faced an enormous task. It was called upon to handle the responsibility of dealing with enemy captives while trying to improve the conditions of Americans languishing in enemy prisons. Basically, this chapter will attempt to describe the efforts of Congress, through such instrumentalities as the Board of War and Ordnance and its successors, to alleviate the sufferings of American personnel imprisoned by the British.

As the war accelerated and many Americans became prisoners of war in 1776, the Board of War and Ordnance made two major recommendations to the Congress at the end of that year. The Board suggested that an office of Commissary General of Prisoners be created to provide an administrative arm to assist the Board in its functions. Additionally, the Board of War and Ordnance asked that a special agent, who would reside in New York City, be appointed to try to help the Americans held captive there.[3]

Congress accepted the Board's ideas and moved to enact them. General Washington was instructed to seek an agreement with General William Howe, the Commander in Chief of British forces in the colonies, which would permit an American to reside in the city and to represent the interests of the men detained there.[4] At first General Howe regarded the proposal noncommittally, but he finally agreed to the concept.[5] Before the matter of an agent in New York City was resolved, however, the Congress turned its attention to the recommendation for the appointment of a Commissary General of Prisoners. Congress decided that such a post was desirable and asked Washington to nominate someone for the task. Washington proposed that Elias Boudinot be elected to the office, and Congress seemed receptive to his response. On April 1, 1777, Washington wrote to Boudinot and informed him that he should soon expect official confirmation from the Congress on his appointment as Commissary General of Prisoners.[6]

On April 15, 1777, Congress did choose Elias Boudinot as Commissary General of Prisoners, but it did not clearly define his office and his duties until June 6, 1777.[7] According to the resolution of Congress, Boudinot was to exercise authority, subject to the direction of Congress, the Board of War and Ordnance, and General Washington, over British troops held in American prisons and to negotiate with his British counterpart to ameliorate the hardships of Americans in British prisons.[8] Congress decided to post Boudinot with the rank of Lieutenant Colonel and with the pay of sixty dollars a month plus expenses. Furthermore, he was empowered to assemble a staff to assist him in his duties. Congress ruled that Boudinot's pay was to be retroactive to May 15, 1777, to compensate him for the service he had already rendered while awaiting official definition of his status and pay.[9]

Before Boudinot was officially confirmed as Commissary General of Prisoners, he commenced to function as such. With Washington's support, he proposed to General Howe that Lewis Pintard, a merchant and pre-war resident of New York City, be recognized as his agent to help Americans imprisoned there. He proposed such an arrangement in April of 1777, and he soon received a letter from Joshua Loring, his British counterpart, that such a concept was an acceptable idea.[10] By the middle of May of 1777, Pintard was ready to serve as Boudinot's agent in New York City, but a series of minor disagreements delayed him from actually beginning service as the resident agent until June of 1777.[11] Boudinot and Pintard encountered numerous obstacles in trying to help the American captives in New York. At first Howe was suspicious of Pintard. Apparently, General Howe worried that Pintard might be using the position to engage in espionage, but he finally accepted Pintard as a legitimate adjunct of Boudinot's department. Nevertheless, Boudinot and Loring bickered constantly over Pintard's role as agent to the prisoners, and, from time to time, Pintard's effectiveness was diminished by the continuous quarreling. In spite of all the difficulties, however, aid for the American captives began to arrive in New York City in 1777. Colonel Boudinot, his staff, and Pintard pursued their duties with laudable energy and devotion.

While Boudinot struggled with the problems of trying to care for the British prisoners under his jurisdiction and attempting to aid Americans in British prisons, the Congress became disenchanted with the Board of War and Ordnance. The idea of such an agency was fundamentally sound, but its performance left much to be desired. The Board of War and Ordnance was composed of five members of Congress, and all five men served on other committees. As a result, the Board of War and Ordnance was often slow to respond to the directives of Congress or to the requests of the Commissary General of Prisoners. So, on October 17, 1777, Congress attempted to improve the situation. The Board of War and Ordnance was replaced by a Board of War.[12] The new agency was a five-man board, but only two of the five men could also be members of Congress. The intention of Congress, obviously, was to reduce inefficiency by erecting a new board with a majority of its members serving only in that capacity. Later events certainly vindicated the alterations Congress made on the old Board of War and Ordnance.

Frequent changes in policy, personnel, and agencies occurred during the war as Congress searched for answers to its problems. The creation of the Board of War was a positive accomplishment, and the transition to the new body was carried off smoothly. Elias Boudinot discharged his duties well, but by early 1778 he decided to resign as Commissary General. He resigned for two reasons. After only ten months of official service, he had become exhausted and frustrated by the demands of his office. Furthermore, his personal financial condition had deteriorated since he had assumed the post as Commissary General of Prisoners, and for reasons both public and personal he tendered his resignation to Congress on April 20, 1778.[13] Congress began to search for a replacement for Boudinot, and after several weeks of delay and indecision it selected John Beatty to fill the vacancy on May 28, 1778.[14] As a result of the delay in appointing his successor and of Beatty's need to acquaint himself with his new post, Boudinot did not lay down the burdens of the office of Commissary General of Prisoners until August of 1778.

John Beatty's role as Commissary General of Prisoners was identical to that of his predecessor. Congress did not significantly alter the function of the office of Commissary General of Prisoners, but Beatty proved more successful than Boudinot in dealing with the prisoner of war question. In all fairness to Boudinot, however, it should be pointed out that the British became more receptive to American overtures to improve conditions for the prisoners of war after 1777. In October of 1777 General John Burgoyne and his entire army surrendered at Saratoga, New York, to the American forces led by General Horatio Gates, which resulted in a significant increase in the number of captives held by the colonials. The increase of British personnel in American prisons helped to promote a more cooperative attitude among the British and a desire for some reforms in the manner in which captives were treated. Beatty was an able man, but he also faced better circumstances as well.

The new Commissary General continued the struggle to promote rapid exchange of captives and to improve the lot of Americans sitting in British prisons. During his tenure of office, Beatty conducted most of his business with Joshua Loring or Lord Rawdon. Loring was the British Commissary General for Prisoners, and Lord Rawdon served on General Clinton's staff. Both Loring and Rawdon manifested an interest in improving the environment of the prisoners held by both sides, and they encouraged Beatty to offer ideas and proposals.

Commissary General of Prisoners Beatty scored an impressive victory in the autumn of 1778. Congress, for the first time, voted funds for Beatty to use to pay the debts incurred by American officers living on parole on Long Island and in New York City.[15] Up to this time, American officers had subsisted on whatever funds they could acquire or on credit, and many of them were heavily in debt. The British Army had frequently complained of the mounting debts, and the Congress decided to intervene. Congress voted to allocate specie to pay the bills for room and board for the paroled officers, and Beatty immediately entered into negotiations with the British to provide for disbursement of the funds.[16] The negotiations quickly bore fruit.

On November 26, 1778, Beatty and Loring agreed that Lewis Pintard would be permitted to use the alloted funds to pay the delinquent bills of the officers, provided the money was in specie and distributed under the general supervision of an officer appointed by Lord Rawdon.[17] The agreement did reduce some of the friction between the two sides, and it signalled a new, more cooperative attitude coming into the foreground. The actual conditions of the officers changed little, but they now did not have to fear being returned to one of the sugar house prisons due to a lack of money to pay their creditors. Basically, however, the agreement to allow funds to reach the paroled American officers had other meanings to Beatty. It appeared that the status of Pintard as an agent was firmly established, and, at the same time, the door was left ajar to discuss other sources of aid for the American captives. Beatty was, however, mistaken about the unqualified acceptance of Pintard by the British.

After approximately a year and one-half of service as Commissary General of Prisoners, Beatty decided to resign his position. On February 23, 1780, Beatty wrote to General Washington and informed him that he intended to leave his post.[18] Beatty declared in his letter to Washington that the "declining state" of his family prompted his decision. As was the case with many of his fellow officers, Beatty was caught in the squeeze brought by the low pay of the continental officers, the inflation in prices and currency, and the inability to cope with them effectively while in uniform. Additionally, of course, the burdens of his office were enormous, and the prospect of escaping them undoubtedly enhanced the thought of resignation. On February 25, 1780, Beatty wrote to Samuel Huntington, the President of the Continental Congress, and stated that he was forwarding his resignation to Congress through the appropriate military channels.[19] Finally, on March 31, 1780, Beatty officially terminated his service as Commissary General of Prisoners.[20] Beatty's administration of the office of Commissary General of Prisoners was a productive one. Exchanges of captives became more frequent under his direction, and greater quantities of money and provisions reached American captives through his efforts.

Congress commenced the search for a new Commissary General of Prisoners shortly after Beatty's resignation was formally accepted. The choice of a new Commissary General was not forthcoming until September 15, 1780, when Abraham Skinner was chosen to fill the vacancy.[21] During the time between Beatty's resignation and Skinner's appointment, the Board of War and General Washington cooperated in handling the correspondence and negotiations concerning the welfare of the prisoners.

The chief item under discussion during the interval between Beatty and Skinner, aside from the usual arguments over the exchange and welfare of captives, revolved about the issue of the resident agents who represented the interests of the prisoners to their captors. Washington personally intervened to try to settle the matter. On March 27, 1780, Washington wrote to Baron von Knyphausen, one of Clinton's staff officers, that Lewis Pintard had assumed the duty of the American resident agent at New York City in the early part of 1777,[22] but he went on to point out that Pintard had never been formally recognized as such by either Howe or Clinton. As a result, he claimed that Pintard's effectiveness had been greatly hindered.[23] On this point, General Washington was correct. In a subsequent letter to Knyphausen, General Washington asked if some sort of formal agreement could be negotiated to permit resident agents to receive recognition and acceptance of their roles as men dedicated to assisting their countrymen.[24] Knyphausen replied favorably and requested that Washington submit a concrete proposal for such an arrangement.[25]

Washington promptly responded to Knyphausen's invitation to offer a plan of some sort. According to Washington's proffered statement, the following regulations were to be employed. An agent would be permitted to dwell by himself or with his family, if he had one, and he would be secure in person and property. The agent would be allowed to visit the prisons once a week to see the prisoners, to tend to their needs, and to listen to their complaints. Additionally, the agent would be allowed to receive money, clothing, and provisions and to distribute them among the prisoners. An agent would be granted the privilege of passing through lines, subject to the approval of the Commander in Chief in whose lines he was located, in search of articles needed by the prisoners of war and allowed to return with the items. In the case of improper conduct on the part of an agent, he could be recalled and a replacement could be automatically named to fill the vacancy. If an agent was recalled, he, his family, and his property were to be permitted to return to friendly lines under a flag of truce. Finally, each Commander in Chief was ultimately answerable for the conduct of his agent.[26] All in all, Washington's plan was a good one; one that merited careful study.

General Clinton received the Washington plan and referred it to General von Knyphausen for study. Knyphausen analyzed the statement carefully and recommended that it be accepted. So on November 4, 1780, the status of the resident agent was finally established.[27] Washington's next step was to notify Pintard of the accord and to ask him to begin to conform to the new rules, but he encountered unexpected opposition from that worthy gentleman. Pintard was exhausted, and he had come to fear for his personal safety.[28] Washington tried to persuade him to continue as his agent, but Pintard refused. Washington asked him to recommend someone to take his place, and Pintard suggested the name of John Franklin. Washington offered the post to Franklin in a letter dated December 28, 1780, and on January 10, 1781, Franklin accepted the assignment.[29] Washington was pleased with the agreement with the British and saddened by the loss of the services of Pintard. Franklin proved to be no less able or dedicated than Pintard, and the new agent discharged his duties well.

While General Washington negotiated a'settlement of the issue of the resident agent, the Congress embarked upon an examination of the accomplishments and shortcomings of the Board of War. After considerable investigation, the Congress decided to abolish the Board of War and to replace it with a War Department.[30] On February 6, 1781, the Congress voted to establish the War Department headed by a Secretary at War.[31] The War Department was given many responsibilities, and among them it was directed to assume all functions relevant to prisoners of war. Major General Benjamin Lincoln was chosen as the Secretary at War. When he entered office in early 1782, he exercised all administrative authority over the prisoner of war question until the war ended.

Throughout the conflict Congress made many changes in agencies and personnel while attempting to cope with the troublesome issue of prisoners of war. The alterations were, for the most part, necessary, but changes in policy, personnel, and departments often contributed to the discomfort of the captives. Nevertheless, the Congress did its best to help the prisoners, and it made halting progress toward that end.

As mentioned in an earlier chapter, the standard British policy was to issue American captives two-thirds the daily food ration alloted to the British soldier and periodically to issue new clothing and bedding. The food allotments were faithfully issued to the men. While the food was alloted regularly, it was often of poor quality and it certainly was a monotonous fare at best. Prisoners especially desired fresh vegetables and fruits, when in season, and other items to vary their diet. If a captive had money he was allowed to purchase extra rations, but most men had little money or their funds were soon exhausted.[32] The American captives were not starved, but they were forced, without outside help, to endure upon a diet that was meager and not very healthful. In addition to their need for better rations, the captives normally lacked adequate bedding and clothing which were exceedingly expensive to purchase. The supplies the American prisoners received from their captor were only adequate at the best. So a plan to augment the prisoners rations, clothing, and bedding was developed by the Congress under the administration of the Commissary General of Prisoners.

As early as June 25, 1776, General Washington began to fret over reports concerning the needs of American captives.[33] Then, as the New York campaign was concluded and thousands of Americans were captured, Washington's concern became acute. In November of 1776, in response to Washington's plea, the Congress appropriated eight thousand dollars for him to use to inaugurate a program of providing aid to the captives detained in New York City.[34] The eight thousand dollars was a modest beginning, but it marked the first effort of Congress to try to relieve the hardships of American prisoners of war. The money was delivered to General Washington, who then managed to secure Howe's permission to send it into New York City for distribution among the men imprisoned there. Obviously, such a small sum did little to bring general relief among the captives, but it was only the first phase of a concerted effort to help them.

Congress was truly concerned over the reports of the hardships faced by the American prisoners of war, and on January 3, 1777, it instructed Washington to propose to General Howe that the two commanders agree that supplies be permitted to reach the prisoners on a regular basis.[35] General Howe responded promptly to Washington's request, refusing to enter into such an arrangement. Howe was suspicious of the proposal, and he also believed such an idea to be an affront to the British Army.[36] Finally, however, he relented, and by May of 1777, provisions began to flow into New York City on an intermittent basis.[37]

On January 18, 1777, Washington again asked Congress to provide money or bills of exchange for distribution among the men held captive in New York City.[38] At this juncture Congress engaged itself in a lengthy debate concerning the wisdom of such a commitment, and it finally decided to comply with Washington's request. A number of appropriations were made in 1777 to advance funds for the relief of the prisoners in British prisons.[39] By April of 1777, Boudinot, who at that point was the acting Commissary General of Prisoners, had been charged with the task of receiving the funds and transmitting them to the prisoners.[40] Although Boudinot's status had not yet been carefully defined, he was hard at work trying to assist his unfortunate countrymen.

At first, the emphasis was placed upon attempting to provide the prisoners with money so they could purchase the items they needed,[41] and all manner of difficulties arose. Congress tried to use paper money to fund the prisoners, but that did not work out well. The captives discovered that local people were disinclined to accept continental currency or would exchange it at an extremely unfavorable rate. The amount of specie available to the Congress was limited, and so it used a combination of paper money, bills of credit or exchange, and specie to send to the captives. Congress finally decided that the emphasis of its aid program to the prisoners needed to be shifted. Money was to be sent to the captives, but Congress began to stress the wisdom of sending food, clothing, and other items to the prisoners. So in the latter part of 1777, the captives began to receive goods of all kinds to be used, bartered, or sold. The burden of trying to supply financial aid exclusively to the prisoners was more than the Congress could manage.

In August of 1777, Boudinot's department was provided with five hundred barrels of flour by the Congress, and he was ordered to send it to New York City. The flour was to be delivered in care of Lewis Pintard, who was to sell it locally and to use the proceeds to help the prisoners.[42] After several delays the flour arrived, and Pintard sold it to raise money to distribute among the captives.[43] The transportation of provisions to New York was a slow business, and, of course, once the goods arrived considerable time elapsed before they could be sold and money could reach the prisoners. The men had little immediate use for five hundred barrels of flour, and Pintard had to make the best sale he could arrange. Such an approach left a good deal to be desired, but Congress had to employ whatever resources it could draw upon. Flour was in demand in New York City, but Pintard's bargaining position was not always enviable, as his prospective customers realized that he was anxious to make a quick sale. Had Pintard had the luxury of waiting longer, he probably could have sold the flour at higher prices. Pintard's deep concern for the plight of the prisoners would not, however, allow him to wait very long to transact his business.

A more substantial accomplishment was achieved with the onset of the winter of 1777. With the coming of cold weather, Boudinot, with the approval and assistance of Congress and General Washington, placed emphasis upon supplying the captives with clothing. He was able to deliver 796 pairs of shoes, 1,310 pairs of stockings, 787 coats, 1,253 shirts, 549 vests, 376 pairs of trousers, 184 hats, 616 blankets, and eight mattresses to the officers and men imprisoned in New York.[44] The lack of sufficient clothing in the winter months was critical for the men, and Boudinot's efforts made the season a bit more comfortable for several hundred men. Much more clothing could have been used by the men, but, as usual, the resources were limited.

The efforts to help the prisoners in New York City went on unabated, but the latter part of 1777 witnessed the appearance of a new problem. General Howe captured Philadelphia in October of 1777, and a new group of captives demanded Boudinot's attention. On November 25, 1777, a sum of money was sent into Philadelphia, with Joshua Loring's permission, to relieve some of the distress of the American captives situated there.[45] In addition to money, Colonel Boudinot sent as much food as he could to the Philadelphia prisoners. For example, he reported to Richard Peters, the Secretary of the Board of War, that he had sent flour, cornmeal, firewood, and twenty-four head of cattle to the captives in Philadelphia by January 11, 1778.[46] Between January and June of 1778, Boudinot sent 857 barrels of flour into the city of Philadelphia to be sold to raise cash for the captives,[47] and, at the same time, he also sent 118 head of cattle and four hogs to supply them with fresh meat.[48] The British soon evacuated Philadelphia in June of 1778, and Boudinot's responsibilities there ended with the withdrawal of the enemy. Not enough food, clothing, and other items reached the prisoners in Philadelphia, but without Boudinot's assistance they would have experienced much greater deprivation.

Most of Boudinot's labors to provision the American prisoners were focused on New York City. By May of 1778 he had shipped a total of 3,741 barrels of flour to New York to be sold for the benefit of the Americans detained there.[49] Additionally, Boudinot continued to send whatever sums of money Congress made available to him for the captives. On August 8, 1778, for instance, he sent ten thousand pounds to Lewis Pintard. Pintard was to reimburse the merchants who had sold food, clothing, and bedding for the prisoners to him on credit, and the remaining funds were to be distributed among the captives.[50] Such a large sum of money was, however, the exception rather than the rule. Ordinarily, Boudinot and Pintard had to employ considerable genius to raise such funds.

In the latter part of 1778, John Beatty replaced Elias Boudinot as the Commissary General of Prisoners, and he continued the program designed to aid the captives. In October and November of 1778, the Congress set aside sums of money for the relief of the prisoners, and Beatty assumed the task of delivering it to them.[51] Beatty also continued the policy of sending flour, beef, pork, firewood, and clothing to New York City for distribution among the Americans incarcerated there.[52] The supplies and money sent into New York were always placed in the hands of all classifications of prisoners. When food, money, or clothing reached Pintard he distributed it among American army and naval personnel, enlisted and commissioned ranks, with an even and honest hand.

Most of the prisoners appreciated the service rendered to them by Boudinot, Beatty, Skinner, Pintard, and Franklin, but they were not above complaining. The prisoners constantly asked for money rather than provisions. Money was much more useful than flour or some other commodity because it could be used to fill a specific need, whereas a new shirt would have to be sold or bartered if the prisoner did not need it.[53] Beatty and Boudinot preferred handling money as aid for the captives. Money was easier to deliver, required no freight expenses, and did more immediate good for the men.

During the Beatty administration, Congress returned to the policy of sending money to the captives in larger quantities.[54] Sending provisions was good, but Congress was horrified at how much of the profit of a shipment of flour, for example, was consumed in paying for its transportation through enemy lines to the prison sites. Congress usually sent paper money to the captives in the early days of the war, which did not prove productive. But in 1778, Congress developed a new scheme to make the paper currency more valuable. Food was in short supply in New York City by 1778, and the prices were outrageously high. So Congress ruled that anyone who exchanged specie for paper, to accommodate the prisoners, would be permitted to enter American lines to buy food where the supply was greater and the prices more reasonable. Many New York residents proved eager to exchange specie for paper and to enter the American lines to buy food.[55] A source of hard money was developed that way, but the men in the prisons still had to pay the local prices for food, which did not benefit them as much as the Congress hoped. Nevertheless, a little progress was made by a fairly simple expedient.

Beatty found the position of Commissary General of Prisoners an easier assignment than did Boudinot. During Boudinot's administration most of the principles governing the provisioning of the prisoners were established by debate, correspondence, and daily practice. Much of Boudinot's time was consumed by his search for an agreement with Joshua Loring, his British counterpart, concerning the rules and regulations regarding supplemental aid to the captives. Beatty was spared that frustrating experience, and his duties were a bit more pleasant as a result. Moreover, Beatty served as the Commissary General at a time when the number of Americans held captive was comparatively small. Beatty had fewer men to assist than did his predecessor. This does not mean that Beatty's term as Commissary General was one without difficulties, but the scale of frustration was less. Beatty was no less able or dedicated than Boudinot, and the prisoners were well served by his occupancy of office. Finally, Beatty resigned his position as Commissary General of Prisoners in March of 1780. Congress did not replace him until September of that year. General Washington assumed the duty of superintending the relief program for the prisoners until Colonel Abraham Skinner was chosen to serve as the new Commissary General.

The events of 1780 were to place a much greater burden upon the new Commissary General than Beatty experienced. Beatty's term of office coincided with a lull in the war, but Colonel Skinner came to his post in the year that the war took on a much more active phase. In the spring of 1780, the city of Charleston, South Carolina, was captured, and with its surrender several thousand prisoners were taken by the British. General Washington immediately inaugurated a program to send relief for the prisoners held in the Charleston vicinity.[56] As soon as Skinner was designated as the new Commissary General of Prisoners, Washington gratefully relinquished the task of supplying the prisoners in Charleston and New York to him. Colonel Skinner performed admirably as the new Commissary General. He was provided with the same tools to assist the prisoners as had been employed by Boudinot and Beatty. Congress issued bills of exchange or credit, appropriated money, purchased provisions and supplies, and directed Skinner to see to the delivery and distribution of the assistance among the captives.[57] In most ways, Skinner's activities were essentially routine in character. One new aspect did appear, however, during his tenure of office. While Skinner was furnished with the same sort of aid that the Congress had given his predecessors in his office, he began to draw upon the states for additional sources of relief for the captives.

Several states began to cooperate with the Congress in attempting to aid American captives in late 1780 and early 1781. In October of 1780, the state of New York sent two hundred barrels of flour into New York City to be sold so the proceeds could be used by Pintard for distribution among the captives.[58] Maryland and Virginia shipped such items as money, firewood, tobacco, and food supplies to New York City for the men detained there.[59] The amount of state sponsored aid was not great, but it was an encouraging turn of events for the Congress and Skinner. Congress decided to try to mobilize additional state participation and requested that all the states issue bills of credit for Skinner to use, but the idea, unfortunately, never enjoyed great success.[60]

Virginia and Maryland were particularly active in the state aid relief program for the captives held in Charleston.[61] In November of 1780 the British granted Governor Thomas Jefferson of Virginia permission to send £5,000 to Charleston for the relief of American prisoners detained in South Carolina.[62] Encouraged by the cooperative attitude of the British, Virginia and Maryland then sent all kinds of aid to the captives in South Carolina. The two states shipped tobacco, beef, flour, rum, clothing, medicine, and bedding to the men in South Carolina prison camps. The state participation in the relief effort was quite a boon to Skinner's department, which also labored steadily to assist the captives.

The combined efforts of the Congress and the state governments to aid the captives continued until the last of the American captives were repatriated at the conclusion of hostilities. Many faults and shortcomings can be assigned to the relief extended to the captives, but without it the men would have suffered more than they did. The Congress, the states, and the Commissary Generals were never totally satisfied with their efforts, but they did about all that their limited resources would allow.

Congress was never able to supply direct assistance, in any appreciable amount, to American prisoners who were imprisoned outside North

America. A good many seamen, some soldiers, and a few civilians were confined in prisons in Great Britain, the Caribbean Islands, and aboard British warships, and these men were beyond the effective range of congressional assistance. The majority of these captives were detained in Mill and Forton prisons in Great Britain. Fortunately for the men held in Forton and Mill prisons, they were detained under slightly more favorable circumstances than their countrymen located in the prisons of New York, Philadelphia, Charleston, Canada, and elsewhere in North America. Nevertheless, the Congress fretted over the welfare of the men who endured in foreign prisons. Several obstacles prevented Congress from providing aid to the captives located outside North America. The matters of time and distance were nearly impossible to overcome. Congress was poorly informed regarding the numbers, locations, and needs of the men held abroad. Additionally, the resources available to assist the captives were limited, and Congress could not afford to risk precious supplies to loss or seizure while en route to foreign prisons. Furthermore, to send provisions, food, and money into enemy ports required complicated diplomatic agreements which the Congress was unable to establish with Great Britain. As a result, the men in the foreign prisons had to depend upon their captors for the bulk of their support.

American personnel confined in foreign prisons were placed under the jurisdiction of the Commissioners for Sick and Hurt Seamen and the Exchange of Prisoners, and they were regularly issued clothing, food, and bedding. The amount of food and other items alloted the captives was adequate, but the men always sought funds to purchase extra food and minor luxuries. Most of the supplemental aid which reached the prisoners came from sources not sponsored directly by the Congress. As mentioned earlier, captives were permitted to receive gifts of money from generous British subjects, relatives and friends, and visitors to the prisons. They also were allowed to barter for goods, to sell whatever items they could manufacture, and to accept charity to raise funds to buy items they desired. The results of all these means depended upon a combination of luck and initiative, and the returns were variable and often disappointing. An aggressive captive might occasionally fare well, but he had little control over his fate most of the time. Prison officials were, however, tolerant of nearly all the enterprises of the captives so long as they did not threaten discipline or prison security.

The only aid the men in foreign nations received from their government came as a result of the efforts of Benjamin Franklin. As a diplomatic envoy to France, Franklin made a few token gestures to assist the captives although his resources to do so were severely limited. In October of 1777

Franklin wrote to David Hartley, a member of Parliament who took a friendly interest in the American captives, and asked him to visit Mill and Forton prisons to distribute small sums of money to the inmates.[63] Hartley proved helpful; he did visit the prisons, and he gave a hundred pounds to the men.[64] Hartley's activities were conducted on an unofficial level, and he depended upon Franklin's honor for repayment — which was forthcoming. Encouraged by Hartley's helpful attitude, Franklin endeavored to establish an agreement with the British government to permit regular assistance for the captives, but he failed to succeed.[65] From 1777 through 1782 Franklin and the Congress had to assist the prisoners in Great Britain through whatever indirect and discreet channels they could develop, which were never satisfactory to either party. In addition to Hartley, Franklin relied heavily upon Thomas Wren, a Presbyterian minister and resident of Portsmouth, England, and William Hodgson, a London merchant, to serve as his messengers to the prisoners.[66] Franklin sent small sums of money periodically, but on the whole the amount of assistance provided to the men was negligible. Wren and Hodgson rendered valuable service to Franklin, and had Franklin possessed greater funds to use, they would have been of enormous benefit to the men held captive.[67]

Throughout the war Congress debated the wisdom of a policy of retaliation upon British captives to improve the conditions of American prisoners. Threats of retaliation or actual retaliation were, in the opinion of Congress, one of the few direct means available to coerce the British into alleviating the rigors of prison life endured by American personnel. A program of retaliation was fraught with peril, and Congress approached it with care. Retaliation upon British personnel might produce positive results or it might enrage the British government and worsen the lives of the American prisoners. In an effort to help the captive Americans and to avoid exposing them to reprisals, Congress acted deliberately and openly upon the issue of retaliation.

At first Congress feared that American prisoners would simply be treated as rebels and executed. Congress and General Washington initiated a campaign in mid-1775 seeking an agreement with the British Army that captured Americans be accorded the status of prisoners of war. Such an agreement would, of course, forestall precipitate action against the captives. General Gage, the British Commander in Chief at that point, and his successors refused to recognize captured Americans as prisoners of war, but they proceeded to treat them as such anyway. By mid-1776, Congress was generally convinced that, while Americans were not officially defined as prisoners of war, Great Britain would not punish them for treason. The Congress then began an aggressive campaign to ease the hardships of the men in British prisons.

Beginning in August of 1775, the endeavor to protect the American personnel from vindictive treatment got underway. General Washington wrote to General Gage and assured him that the few captured British personnel in his custody were well treated, but that their conditions would be regulated in the future by the treatment American personnel received from their captors.[68] Washington's letter to Gage might appear innocuous, but it was, in fact, a significant exploratory step. A few weeks later Congress moved to reinforce Washington's warning to Gage. Congress voted that all British captives be provisioned in amounts equal to those issued to American prisoners by the British authorities.[69] In both actions, the intent was clear. General Washington and the Congress wished to establish an understanding of some sort to govern treatment of captives, but they also indicated their willingness to adopt harsh measures toward British troops to define and enforce an agreement. General Gage remained silent while Washington and Congress worried over the possible fate of the captives. Gage would not commit himself to any arrangement since he did not expect the conflict to continue for any appreciable length of time. As the prospect for an early end to the war waned in 1776, tacit agreement between the belligerents regarding rules of conduct toward the prisoners emerged. The British Army was in a delicate situation. Any agreement with the rebels was out of the question as it might be construed as a recognition of the legitimacy of the American Army, something that both the British Army and London wished to avoid. About all that Gage, Howe, Clinton, and Carleton could do was to set an example and to hope that the Americans would be satisfied and respond in kind.

General William Howe, Gage's replacement as Commander in Chief, landed his army on Staten Island in the summer of 1776, and he commenced the struggle to regain control of New York for the Crown. Howe's brilliantly successful effort produced several thousand American captives. At that point, Congress and General Washington began to labor tirelessly in the quest for an understanding governing prisoner welfare. Officially, Howe remained aloof and did not enter into any direct negotiations, but he clearly intended to treat the captives as prisoners of war. He seemed to hope that his intentions were understood by the Congress. All the discussion, such as it was, between Howe and the American authorities meant little in the early months of the war since few British troops had fallen into American hands. That changed, however, in December of 1776. General Washington won a quick victory at Trenton, New Jersey, right after Christmas and several hundred Hessian mercenaries were captured. The victory at Trenton was a significant one for colonial morale, but it also supplied the Congress with the pawns it needed to maneuver for better conditions for American captives.[70]

Congress chose to use the case of General Charles Lee to demonstrate its determination to employ retaliation as a means to secure redress for American captives. General Lee was taken captive in New Jersey after the defense of New York had collapsed in 1776. General Lee, a Continental officer and former British Army officer, was subjected to harsh treatment when first imprisoned. Congress was truly concerned about Lee, and it offered an exchange for him. Howe declined the offer of an exchange, and Congress feared the worst for General Lee. When it became clear that Howe had no immediate interest in exchanging Lee, the Congress ordered that six enemy officers be placed under close confinement and accorded the same treatment as Lee received.[71] The six officers were not treated harshly, but they were the first official examples of retaliation.[72] Ultimately, Lee was exchanged in 1778, and Congress won a small victory.

Even though Lee was finally offered for an exchange, the Congress remained unhappy over the conditions of American captives. Washington again warned Howe that he was prepared to retaliate upon British officers if conditions in the British prisons were not improved.[73] The American authorities usually concentrated their threats of retaliation upon the officers because most members of Congress had no objection to retaliating upon commissioned officers. They did, however, oppose employing retaliatory measures upon enlisted men for fear it might enrage the British public.[74] The protests about the treatment of the American captives continued throughout 1777, but the only retaliatory measures sanctioned by the Congress were close confinement of selected officers and equalization of rations issued to the British prisoners to reflect those received by American captives. At the close of 1777, however, Congress began to hint that a much broader policy of retaliation would be employed if Howe did not improve the environment of American captives.[75] Congress was convinced that a policy of retaliation, to prove successful, required a threat of massive retaliation upon all British personnel under American jurisdiction.

Congress began to discuss a shift in policy in early 1778. Only a limited number of British officers had been subjected to retaliation so far, but Congress was not pleased with the results. Additionally, General John Burgoyne's army had been captured at Saratoga, New York, in late 1777, and Congress had a fresh supply of prisoners to use as pawns in the struggle to secure better treatment for American prisoners of war. Congress opened a debate upon a report from the Board of War which recommended that a policy of general retaliation upon all captured British personnel be commenced immediately.[76] The Board of War report urged that the rations of all enemy prisoners be reduced until American captives experienced an improvement in their lives.[77] Finally, on January 21, 1778, the Congress voted to accept the Board of War recommendation, and it directed the Commissary General of Prisoners to reduce the daily food allotment for all enemy captives and to confine them under conditions equal to those endured by American prisoners.[78] Congress elected to increase the pressure upon the British Army in 1778 to protect American prisoners from further suffering, but the Congress, in essence, moved cautiously.

Congress followed through on its decision to enforce stricter regulations upon British captives in 1778. Rations were reduced, and a sizeable number of British personnel were placed under close confinement. And then, to underscore its resolve, Congress voted on November 7, 1778, to continue the policy of treating British captives in a manner equal to that received by Americans in British prisons.

For the next three years, the policy of retaliation upon British prisoners, based upon the resolution of January 21, 1778, continued in a sporadic fashion. Normally, during the period of 1778 through 1781 the restrictions placed upon British captives were of short duration. Retaliatory measures, such as food reductions or close confinement, were relaxed after a few weeks or sooner if Congress received intelligence that Americans had witnessed an improvement in their conditions in the prisons. Congress was content to threaten action, but it acted with restraint when reprisals were ordered. After several years of limited and cautious retaliation, Congress became disenchanted with its success, and, in January of 1781, a more comprehensive plan of retaliation was approved.[79]

Abraham Skinner, the Commissary General of Prisoners, was directed to reduce the food allotments again.[80] The difference this time was that the reductions were to be permanent until further notice from Congress or the Board of War. In the earlier program of retaliation, the Commissary General had possessed the power to decide when the British captives were to be returned to normal food allotments. The Commissary Generals of Prisoners were humane men and they usually seized upon the first evidence of improved conditions for Americans to ease the restrictions placed upon the British captives, and, evidently, Congress was convinced that Boudinot, Beatty, and Skinner were inclined to be too easy on the prisoners.

After several months of observing the effects of the renewed pressure, the War Department ordered on June 11, 1781, that the restrictions were to continue until it was satisfied that Great Britain had improved the lot of American prisoners. There is little evidence that any of the measures adopted by the Congress produced much success in ameliorating the hardships of American captives. Congress was aware, however, that its stern pronouncements were not without their propaganda value, and it maintained a steady flow of criticism and threats regarding the matter of prisoner welfare.

One incident involving the execution of an American officer nearly opened the door to a series of ugly reprisals. Captain Joshua Huddy of the New Jersey Militia was the victim of one of the most bizarre incidents of the Revolution. Huddy commanded a blockhouse on Toms River in New Jersey which was attacked by a detachment of Loyalist troops on March 23-24, 1782.[81] After a bitter skirmish, Huddy was forced to surrender to the raiders, and he and his men were taken to New York City as prisoners of war. Huddy and his comrades were the captives of an organization known as the Associated Loyalists, who were headquartered in New York City. The Associated Loyalists were a special military force recruited from among men displaced by the war. Their function was to harass the rebels.[82] The Associated Loyalists, paid and equipped by the British, were under the nominal command of the British Army. They operated under the immediate supervision of an agency composed of Tories known as the Board of Associated Loyalists. At the time of the atrocity, the President of the Board of Associated Loyalists was William Franklin.[83] While the Refugees, as they styled themselves, were technically under the command of Henry Clinton, they frequently engaged in operations without his prior knowledge or consent. The Huddy tragedy arose from the loose chain of command.

Upon their arrival in New York City, Huddy and his men were placed in the Provost, where the Refugees were allowed to keep their captives until they could be offered in an exchange of prisoners. Huddy expected that he and his men would eventually be returned to their homes. Destiny was not that kind to Captain Huddy. A refugee named Philip White was captured in New Jersey by the state militia while visiting his wife who still lived there. Then, under circumstances which are unclear, White was killed. His captors claimed he was shot while trying the escape.[84] The death of Philip White sealed the fate of Captain Joshua Huddy. On April 12, 1782, a party of Refugees, under the command of Captain Richard Lippincot, landed in New Jersey and hanged Huddy. A note was pinned to Huddy's coat which declared:

> We, the Refugees, have with grief long beheld the cruel murders of our brethren, and finding nothing but such measures daily carrying into execution, we, therefore, determine not to suffer without taking vengeance for the numerous cruelties,

and having made use of Captain Huddy as the first object to present to your view, and further determine to hang man for man, as long as a refugee is left existing. UP GOES HUDDY FOR PHILIP WHITE.[85]

Congress was faced with the most blatant act of premeditated cruelty on record during the Revolution. The murder of Captain Huddy touched off an acrimonious quarrel.

General Clinton was horrified when he learned of Huddy's death, and he hastened to investigate the whole episode. Clinton was angered by the action of the Refugees. He felt that Britain had been dishonored by the execution, and he also feared for the safety of his men held in American prisons.[86] Clinton's concern was genuine, and his fears were not unfounded. Upon learning of Huddy's death, General Washington wrote to Sir Henry Clinton demanding that Lippincot be remanded to American authorities or appropriate reprisal would be taken.[87] Clinton was well acquainted with American threats of retaliation, and, in this case, he was certain that the danger of reprisal was real. Sir Henry acted quickly to avert a bloodbath of reprisals. He ordered Captain Lippincot be placed under arrest, and he directed that all captives of the Associated Loyalists be transferred to his immediate jurisdiction so that he could vouch for their safety.[88]

As Clinton began an investigation of the atrocity, General Washington, with the approval of Congress, ordered that a British officer be chosen by lot and sent to Philadelphia.[89] If necessary, Washington intended to hang the British officer in retaliation for Huddy. Captain Charles Asgill of the First Foot Guards, who was only twenty years old, drew the fateful lot and was sent to Philadelphia. By the summer of 1782, the situation was tense. Young Asgill, who had been taken prisoner when Lord Cornwallis surrendered at Yorktown, was totally innocent of any crime. No one, including Washington relished the burgeoning disaster.[90]

In the meantime, Sir Henry Clinton was replaced as Commander in Chief by Sir Guy Carleton. Carleton ordered a court martial of Captain Lippincot, and, after several weeks of trial, Lippincot was found innocent of murder. The court condemned Lippincot's action, but stated it believed that he had hanged Huddy because he thought he had been verbally ordered so to do.[91] The Board of Associated Loyalists was generally thought responsible for issuing an ambiguous command which Lippincot had misinterpreted, although no action was taken against the Board or any of its members. The burden of the Court's opinion was that the Board of Loyalists was poorly organized and directed and for those reasons the tragedy had occurred. Captain Lippincot's acquittal of murder closed the matter for the British Army. With Lippincot's dismissal, however, the matter was not necessarily closed. Certainly many innocent men were vulnerable to vicious reprisal if Asgill was put to death. Congress, however, decided not to execute Captain Asgill. Fortunately, for Asgill, Congress, and others, the French government intervened in Asgill's behalf. Lady Asgill, the young officer's mother, wrote to Comte de Vergennes, the French Foreign Minister, and begged him to prevent her only son from being put to death.[92] Vergennes, who was moved by the letter, was also mindful of the fact that many Frenchmen were now prisoners of war in British prisons. Vergennes wrote to General Washington and requested that Asgill be spared and that no other reprisal be taken.[93] After considerable debate, Congress reprieved Asgill and ordered that he be set free and sent to New York City.[94] Washington informed Vergennes that Asgill had been set free and complimented him for his humanity and intercession at the propitious moment.[95] Young Asgill's plight had deeply distressed General Washington, and he did not want to carry out the threat by executing him.

The Huddy-Lippincot affair was a tragedy of the worst kind, and it amply illustrated the rancor which developed in the course of the war. But it also demonstrated that the belligerents did not take leave of their senses either. Washington, Clinton, Carleton, and the Congress all acted with restraint. Senseless acts of cruelty occurred during the Revolution, but they were unusual. Neither side carried out premeditated programs of vicious reprisals upon their captives. When men did suffer at the hands of their captors, the suffering usually resulted from neglect or from the acts of ignorant, unsupervised men. The British Army did not officially condone mistreatment of its captives, but it was often guilty of neglect of the prisoners or the failure to supervise properly the men who were charged to look after the captives — a not unusual situation even in more recent wars.

FOOTNOTES

[1] JCC, IV, 361.

[2] *Ibid.*, V, 434-35. PCC, Roll 72, Item 59, I-II, 45.

[3] PCC, Roll 72, Item 59, I-II, 47.

[4] General Howe to General Washington, January 20, 1777, BHQP, Reel 3, Document 392. JCC, VII, 41.

[5] Joshua Loring to Elias Boudinot, April 24, 1777, J. J. Boudinot, ed., *The Life, Public Services, and Letters of Elias Boudinot, L.L.D., President of the Continental Congress* (Cambridge, Massachusetts, 1896), I, 46. Cited hereafter as Boudinot, *Life of Boudinot.*

[6] Washington to Boudinot, April 1, 1777, Washington Papers, Library of Congress, Washington, D. C., Reel 40. Cited hereafter as Washington Papers.

[7] Washington to Boudinot, April 15, 1777, *ibid.*, Reel 41. PCC, Roll 72, Item 59, I-II, 48. Boudinot, *Life of Boudinot*, I, 42-43.

[8] *Ibid.*

[9] Boudinot, *Life of Boudinot*, April 24, 1777, I, 43-53.

[10] Loring to Boudinot, *ibid.*, 46.

[11] Lewis Pintard to Elias Boudinot, May 19, 1777, Boudinot Papers. Washington to Board of War and Ordnance, June 6, 1777, Fitzpatrick, *Writings of Washington*, VIII, 191.

[12] JCC, X, 646.

[13] Boudinot, *Life of Boudinot*, I, 110-11. PCC, Roll 72, Item 59, I-II, 52.

[14] JCC, XI, 546. Beatty was chosen on April 28, 1778.

[15] John Beatty to Joshua Loring, October 10, 1778, Clinton Papers.

[16] Lord Rawdon to Colonel Beatty, November 25, 1778, and John Beatty to Lord Rawdon, November 26, 1778, *ibid.*

[17] Agreement Relative to the Money for the Discharge of the Board of Officers on Parole, November 26, 1778, *ibid.*

[18] John Beatty to George Washington, February 23, 1780, Washington Papers, Reel 64.

[19] John Beatty to Samuel Huntington, February 25, 1780, PCC, Roll 91, Item 78, III, 437.

[20] *Ibid.*, Roll 72, Item 59, I-II, 59.

[21] *Ibid.*, 60. JCC, XVIII, 828.

[22] George Washington to Baron von Knyphausen, March 27, 1780, Fitzpatrick, *Writings of Washington*, XVIII, 169.

[23] *Ibid.* The November 26, 1778, agreement between Beatty and Loring failed to secure a formal recognition of Pintard's status as agent for the prisoners. Pintard was allowed to serve the captives, but the British Army remained reluctant to accept him on any sort of formal basis.

[24] George Washington to Baron von Knyphausen, June 1, 1780, *ibid.*, 470-71.

[25] Proposition Respecting Agents for Prisoners, *ibid.*, XIX, 256-57.

[26] *Ibid.*

[27] George Washington to Lewis Pintard, November 9, 1780, *ibid.*

[28] Lewis Pintard to George Washington, December 6, 1780, and December 16, 1780, Washington Papers.

[29] George Washington to John Franklin, December 28, 1780, and John Franklin to George Washington, January 10, 1781, Fitzpatrick, *Writings of*

Washington, XXI, 26-27, 83.

[30] Edmund Cody Burnett, *The Continental Congress* (New York, 1941), 492.

[31] *Ibid.*, 525. Lincoln officially accepted the appointment on December 10, 1781. JCC, XXI, 1087.

[32] Jonathan Gillet to Elizabeth Gillet, December 2, 1776, Stiles, *Letters from Prisons and Prison Ships*, 11. Most of the men had only paper money, and they had to exchange their paper for specie. The going rate was eight dollars paper for one dollar silver.

[33] Major Return Meigs to George Washington, July 25, 1776, Sparks, *Correspondence*, I, 265.

[34] George Washington to Colonel Miles, November 25, 1776, Force, *American Archives*, III, 838. George Washington to Jonathan Trumbull, December 21, 1776, Fitzpatrick, *Writings of Washington*, VI, 410.

[35] PCC, Roll 72, Item 59, I-II, 47.

[36] General Howe to George Washington, January 29, 1777, BHQP, Reel 3, Document 392.

[37] Joshua Loring to Elias Boudinot, May 19, 1777, and Lewis Pintard to Elias Boudinot, May 19, 1777, Boudinot Papers.

[38] George Washington to President of Congress, January 18, 1777, Fitzpatrick, *Writings of Washington*, VII, 435.

[39] Force, *American Archives*, III, 1564, 1567, 1569, 1580, 1593, 1595.

[40] PCC, Roll 72, Item 59, I - II, 48. George Washington to President of Congress, April 26, 1777, Fitzpatrick, *Writings of Washington*, VII, 476.

[41] Lewis Pintard to Elias Boudinot, May 19, 1777, Boudinot Papers.

[42] John Adams to Elias Boudinot, August 8, 1777, and Lewis Pintard to Elias Boudinot, September 3, 1777, *ibid.*

[43] Lewis Pintard to Elias Boudinot, September 4, 1777, *ibid.*

[44] Return of Clothing by L. Pintard to the Continental Prisoners, November 1777 - January 1778, *ibid.*

[45] Elias Boudinot to Captain Mackenzie, November 25, 1777, BHQP, Reel 3A, Document 758.

[46] Elias Boudinot to Richard Peters, January 11, 1778, PCC, Reel 91, Item 78, II, 339. Elias Boudinot to H. H. Ferguson, January 10, 1778, Boudinot Papers.

[47] Boudinot Ledger, New York Public Library, New York, New York, 69. Cited hereafter as Boudinot Ledger. Robert Caughey to Elias Boudinot, January 6, 1778, Boudinot Papers. The cost of provisions was great. Boudinot figured that wheat cost 12 shillings per bushel, wood cost £3 per cord, and beef cost 7 shillings per pound, *ibid.*

[48] *Ibid.*, 70.

[49] Flour Account, New York, No. 2, *ibid.*, 69.

[50] Lewis Pintard to Elias Boudinot, August 1, 1778, Lewis Pintard Papers, New-York Historical Society, New York, New York. Cited hereafter as Pintard Papers. Elias Boudinot to Lewis Pintard, August 8, 1778, Boudinot Papers.

[51] PCC, Roll 72, Item 59, I-II, 59. JCC, XVIII, 1108.

[52] PCC, Roll 72, Item 59, I-II, 56. Lewis Pintard to Captain Smith, January 1, 1779, BHQP, Reel 5, Document 1655. George Washington to Lord Stirling, January 14, 1779, Fitzpatrick, *Writings of Washington*, XIV, 13. Reminiscences of the Early Life of John Pintard, The New-York Historical Society, New York, New York, 66-70. Cited hereafter as Reminiscences of John Pintard.

[53] JCC, XVI, 15.

[54] *Ibid.*, XV, 1436. For example, between April and November, 1779, Congress provided the Commissary General with $32,998 to aid the captives in New York. Also see Board of War Report, *ibid.*, XII, 934. PCC, Roll 72, Item 59, I-II, 56-58.

[55] Adlum, *Memoirs,* 128. Lewis Pintard to Elias Boudinot, August 1, 1778, Pintard Papers.

[56] PCC, Roll 72, Item 59, I-II, 59, 60, 63. George Washington to John Adams, May 10, 1780, Fitzpatrick, *Writings of Washington*, XVIII, 345. JCC, XVI, 381; XVII, 753; XVIII, 762-63. George Washington to Henry Clinton, September 11, 1780, BHQP, Reel 9, Document 3007.

[57] PCC, Roll 72, Item 59, I-II, 60-61. George Washington to Thomas Jefferson, August 29, 1780, Fitzpatrick, *Writings of Washington*, XIX, 468. JCC, XVII, 906-7.

[58] PCC, Roll 72, Item 59, I-II, 61.

[59] George Washington to Thomas Jefferson, August 29, Fitzpatrick, *Writings of Washington*, XIX, 468. Major Towles to Thomas Jefferson, October 10, 1780, W. P. Palmer, ed., *Calendar of Virginia State Papers and other Manuscripts, 1652-1781* (New York, 1968), I, 378-79. Cited hereafter as Palmer, *Calendar.* Thomas Jefferson to Benjamin Harrison, February 7, 1781, McIlwaine, *Letters*, II, 323-24.

[60] Congress suggested the following quota for each state: New Hampshire $2,319, Massachusetts $13,334, Rhode Island $1,160, Connecticut $9,855, New York $4,347, New Jersey $5,217, Pennsylvania $13,334, Delaware $987, Maryland $9,159, Virginia $14,492, North Carolina $5,796, and nothing for South Carolina or Georgia. Palmer, *Calendar*, I, 421-22.

[61] William Phillips to Thomas Jefferson, November 28, 1780, Boyd, *Papers of Jefferson*, IV, 163-65.

[62] George Washington to Henry Clinton, September 11, 1780, and Henry Clinton to George Washington, November 29, 1780, BHQP, Reel 9, Document 3007 and 3165. George Washington to Henry Clinton, May 16, 1781, Fitzpatrick, *Writings of Washington*, XXII, 92. Charles Scott to Thomas Jefferson, no date, and Thomas Jefferson to David Geddes, February 3, 1781, Boyd, *Papers of Jefferson*, IV, 481-82, 516-17.

[63] Benjamin Franklin to David Hartley, October 14, 1777, Smyth, *Writings of Franklin*, VII, 71-72.

[64] Benjamin Franklin to David Hartley, February 12, 1778, *ibid.*, 101-2. Cutter, "Yankee Privateersman," 348-49.

[65] Benjamin Franklin to Sir Grey Cooper, December 11, 1777, Smyth, *Writings of Franklin*, VII, 76-77.

[66] Cutter, "Yankee Privateersman," 348. JCC, XXVI, 144. President of Congress to Reverend Thomas Wren, November 1, 1783, Burnett, *Letters*, VII, 362. Benjamin Franklin to Robert R. Livingston, June 25, 1782, Smyth, *Writings of Franklin*, VIII, 551.

[67] Congress passed a resolution on March 16, 1784, thanking Hodgson for his humane attention to American prisoners in England, JCC, XXVI, 144. Princeton awarded Wren a Doctor of Divinity for his service to American prisoners of war. Benjamin Franklin to William Hodgson, December 10, 1788, Smyth, *Writings of Franklin*, IX, 124; Catherine M. Prelinger, "Benjamin Franklin And The American Prisoners of War in England During The American Revolution," *The William and Mary Quarterly* Third Series, XXXII (1975), 269. Cited hereafter as Prelinger, "Benjamin Franklin."

[68] George Washington to General Thomas Gage, August 20, 1775, Fitzpatrick, *Writings of Washington*, III, 430-31.

[69] JCC, III, 358. Congress acted on November 11, 1775.

[70] Thatcher, *Journal*, 89. George Washington to William Howe, January 13, 1777, Fitzpatrick, *Writings of Washington*, VII, 1-3.

[71] George Washington to President of Congress, June 14, 1777, Fitzpatrick, *Writings of Washington*, VIII, 242. PCC, Roll 72, Item 59, I-II, 48. JCC, VIII, 430-31.

[72] Henry Laurens to John Lewis Gervais, August 5, 1777, Burnett, *Letters*, II, 438-39.

[73] George Washington to William Howe, November 23, 1777, Fitzpatrick, *Writings of Washington*, X, 97-98. George Washington to Henry Clinton, November 23, 1777, Boudinot Papers.

[74] JCC, X, 76-80.

[75] *Ibid.*

[76] PCC, Roll 72, Item 59, I-II, 51. Henry Laurens to John Laurens,

January 22, 1778, Burnett, *Letters*, III, 48.

[77]Elias Boudinot to Robert Hooper, March 28, 1778, and Robert Hooper to Elias Boudinot, May 9, 1778, Boudinot Papers. JCC, XI, 723.

[78]PCC, Roll 72, Item 59, I-II, 55.

[79]Jesse Root to Governor of Connecticut, January 8, 1781, Burnett, *Letters*, V, 521.

[80]George Washington to Abraham Skinner, February 18, 1781, Fitzpatrick, *Writings of Washington*, XXI, 243-44.

[81]Katherine Mayo, *General Washington's Dilemma* (New York, 1938), 72-74. Cited herafter as Mayo, *Washington's Dilemma*. Boudinot, *Journal*. 60-61.

[82]Larry Bowman, "The Court-Martial of Captain Richard Lippincot," *New Jersey History*, LXXXIX (1971), 25. Cited hereafter as Bowman, "Court-Martial of Lippincot."

[83]*Ibid.*

[84]*Ibid.*, 27.

[85]Boudinot, *Journal*, 60-61. BHQP, Reel 12, Document 4443.

[86]Henry Clinton, *The American Rebellion: Sir Henry Clinton's Narrative of His Campaigns, 1775-1782, with an Appendix of Original Documents*, edited by William B. Willcox (New Haven, Connecticut, 1954), 359-60. Cited hereafter as Clinton, *American Rebellion*. BHQP, Reel 12, Document 4443.

[87]George Washington to Henry Clinton, April 21, 1782, Fitzpatrick, *Writings of Washington*, XXIV, 146-47. PCC, Roll 72, Item 59, I-II, 48-51.

[88]Bowman, "Court-Martial of Lippincot," 29. PCC, Roll 200, Item 194, 23-24.

[89]George Washington to Moses Hazen, May 3, 1782, Fitzpatrick, *Writings of Washington*, XXIV, 217-18.

[90]George Washington to Secretary at War, June 5, 1782, *ibid.*, 319-20. Smyth, *Writings of Franklin*, VIII, 572n.

[91]Bowman, "Court-Martial of Lippincot," 30-36.

[92]Lady Asgill to Count de Vergennes, July 18, 1782, Francis Wharton, ed., *Revolutionary Diplomatic Correspondence* (Washington, D. C., 1889), V, 635-36. Cited hereafter as Wharton, *Revolutionary Diplomatic Correspondence*.

[93]Count de Vergennes to George Washington, July 29, 1782, *ibid.*, 636-37.

[94]JCC, XXIII, 690-91, 715, 719-20.

[95]George Washington to Count de Vergennes, November 21, 1782, Fitzpatrick, *Writings of Washington*, XXV, 359.

chapter five

Paths to Freedom

American prisoners of war soon realized they could anticipate an end to their confinement, short of death, in one of four ways so long as hostilities continued. Escape, enlistment in the British armed forces, parole, or exchange were the means of ending their days in prison. Most men who are captives are obsessed with the thoughts of when and how they will regain their freedom, and American prisoners during the Revolution were no exception. All four paths to freedom were explored.

Escapes and escape attempts from prisons and prison ships were not uncommon, but such bids for freedom required courage and ingenuity. Many prisoners lacked the conviction and genius to attempt an escape. Security in British prisons was not foolproof, but the risks and penalties for those who tried to break out of prison and failed were real and sometimes expensive. Most men are too prudent to try such an avenue to liberty when there is hope of other means. Additionally, if a man elected to escape he had to make the attempt at a time when his physical strength was equal to the tasks such an undertaking presented. The best time for such an attempt was shortly after being captured. Most men soon lacked the requisite strength if they were imprisoned for any length of time, and the longer they delayed the more the chance of success usually declined with the procrastination. Nevertheless, many men, as mentioned in previous chapters, did choose this means to try to set themselves at liberty even though their captors exercised all manner of precautions to forestall escapes. The chronicles of the escapes of prisoners of war present one of the smaller and more heroic aspects of any war. Many brave and determined

Americans made successful escapes from prison during the Revolution.[1]

A number of American military personnnel chose to end their imprisonment by the least honorable alternative open to them. In the latter part of 1776, the British military authorities commenced a program of recruitment from among American captives. The British needed manpower badly, and the captives were a source that was explored and exploited. The British realized that among the captives were men who were desperate to leave the prisons. Some of the prisoners of war lacked conviction in the cause that had led to their imprisonment, and others were simply opportunists; in any event, a body of captives was an attractive possibility to a recruiting officer.

The technique of enlisting American personnel into the British armed forces was not at all a subtle one. Soon after the men were captured they were approached by recruiting officers who emphasized the boredom, disease, and the peril prison life offered and presented the captives with the opportunity to avoid the horrors of long confinement by entering his Majesty's service.

John Adlum, a young Pennsylvania militiaman who was captured at Fort Washington on November 16, 1776, recorded his impressions of the enlistment overtures to American captives.[2] After his capture Adlum and his comrades were marched into New York City and confined in New Bridewell Prison. The day after their arrival a number of British recruiting officers appeared at the prison and tried to persuade the captives to enlist in the British Army.[3] Adlum wrote that the recruiters were unsuccessful that day. According to his account, one boy, a fourteen year old drummer, joined the British Army as a result of the visitation of the recruiters. At the same time that Adlum witnessed attempts to enlist Americans, another American named William Slade also recorded British efforts to recruit American personnel. Slade, an inmate aboard the prison ship *Grovnor*, reported in his diary that twenty prisoners had joined the King's service.[4] Such efforts to recruit from among the Americans captured in the New York campaign of 1776 were common, but apparently they were not very successful.[5] There are no reliable statistics available regarding the number of men who proved receptive to the cajoling of the enemy recruiters. The British recruiting officers promised, if at all possible, to protect the identity of the deserters, a promise which they apparently made good. The only evidence one can find are the fragmentary statements of such men as Adlum and Slade, who recorded the activities of the recruiters. Adlum and Slade provide the first examples one can use to document the enlisting of prisoners of war into his Majesty's armed forces, and even Adlum and Slade did not identify by name the men they knew who joined the British.

While the British efforts to enlist American captives enjoyed only limited success in 1776, George Washington became concerned enough to write to General Howe and officially protest the practice in early 1777.[6] In his letter to Howe, General Washington declared he believed that the conditions the men endured in the prisons were designed to encourage them to desert and join the British Army. General Washington demanded an improvement in the poor conditions of the prisons and a cessation to the practice of enlisting American personnel. Throughout 1777, Washington often voiced the suspicion that American captives were subjected to hardship for the sole purpose of making service in the British armed forces appear more attractive.[7] Frequent protests against the enlistment of captives were lodged by the American authorities, but the practice continued for the duration of the war.

Since a formal protest produced no results, Congress attempted to halt the recruitment practice in other ways. Congress decided to forbid the enlistment of enemy captives or deserters into American armed forces. The Congress hoped that it could set an example which would induce the British to abandon their policy of raising recruits from among the captives. By March of 1778, Congress had made its decision, and General Washington informed the Congress that he was following its instructions.[8] Later in the year, Congress directed Washington to purge his army of enemy captives or deserters recruited prior to 1778.[9] Congress was annoyed by the British policy of enticing Americans into their armed forces, but it was more concerned with improving the difficult conditions under which the American captives existed in prison. Congress was convinced, as was Washington, that the discomfort of the American captives was calculated to induce enlistments. By setting an example of excluding British personnel from serving in American armed forces, the Congress hoped to discourage the practice of recruiting American captives on the part of Great Britain. Then, the logic ran, the treatment accorded the captives would improve once the pressure to enlist in the enemy army or navy was ended. But the British practice of attempting to recruit Americans continued.

American captives, wherever they were located, were offered the opportunity to join his Majesty's forces. For a brief time, from 1778 to 1780, the quarrel over recruiting Americans became less prominent, but in 1780 it was renewed with fresh vigor. In 1780, after the British seized Charleston, South Carolina, the practice of enlisting American personnel was accelerated. Lord George Germain, the Colonial Secretary, officially encouraged Generals Clinton and Cornwallis to recruit actively among the American prisoners of war detained in the Charleston vicinity.[10] Germain's idea was to entice Americans to join the Royal Navy or regiments to be posted in the West Indies and to deploy them in the struggle in the Caribbean against the Spanish.[11] As early as September 25, 1780, Major General Benjamin Lincoln, who had surrendered Charleston to Clinton's invading force, wrote to General Washington that many Americans were deserting to the British to escape the loathsome conditions of the South Carolina prisons.[12] The British offer to the captives of enlisting in his Majesty's forces to serve against the Spanish in the Caribbean produced results. According to one source an estimated five hundred to six hundred men decided to fight the Spanish in the West Indies.[13] Additional recruits for the West Indies forces were forthcoming throughout 1781.[14]

Congress became so exasperated over the continuing policy of enlisting American captives that it made a special investigation of the issue in 1781.[15] In the study, Congress reiterated its belief that the enlistment of prisoners of war was contrary to rules of war, and that the vile living conditions to be found in the Charleston prisons were designed to promote the recruitment of American prisoners into Great Britain's military forces.[16] Congress wearily directed Washington to file another protest against the policy of enlisting American captives and turned its attention to other matters, recognizing defeat on this issue.[17] As far away as Madrid, Spain, John Jay, who was on diplomatic duty there, announced his belief that American captives, wherever they were detained, were subjected to harsh conditions simply to encourage desertion.[18] It became an article of faith among the Patriots that the British used the prisons to promote recruitment. The policy of enlisting Americans into the British forces continued into 1782, and Congress routinely and unsuccessfully remonstrated with the British for their actions.[19]

A good deal of furor accompanied the British policy of accepting American captives as volunteers, if they can be correctly termed volunteers. It should be emphasized, however, that the majority of American captives refused to desert to the British armed forces. The prospect of escaping a prison by simply signing an enlistment paper must have been an inviting temptation to a man who had no reason to expect a speedy release from prison. Nevertheless, the great majority of the captives remained constant to their pledge of loyalty to their cause.

Attempting an escape from a prison or enlisting into the service of Great Britain had their obvious and unattractive features to a prisoner wishing somehow to end his captivity. An escape attempt, even for the most determined prisoner, was not lightly undertaken. The dangers of such a venture were real. A prisoner had to consider the possibility of being killed or seriously injured in such an act. He also had to decide whether the penalties for failure to succeed in an escape effort were worth the risk.

Prisoners were sometimes placed in solitary confinement, had their names placed at the bottom of exchange lists, suffered physical abuse, or received reduced food rations for trying to escape. Many men could not muster the courage to confront such peril.

But enlisting into the armed forces of Great Britain was an unsatisfactory means of fleeing the military prisons. First of all, such a decision was a dishonorable one. Furthermore, a prisoner weighing such a decision had to consider the consequences of his act in terms of the long range effects. What if he were captured by American forces while in British uniform? How would he be treated by his British commanders? What would be his legal status and fate at the conclusion of hostilities? A great many imponderables attended a decision of this sort. Both escape or enlistment offered uncertain results, in the short or long run of events, to a captive. Consequently, only a small portion of American prisoners of war elected to employ one of these means to solve their dilemma.

The most desirable avenue to freedom for a prisoner of war was either to be paroled or repatriated in an exchange of captives. Normally, for a recently taken captive, parole offered the best hope of a quick release from prison. Exchanges of prisoners were slow, complicated, and uncertain. In addition to the tangled political matters which often stalled exchanges, a prisoner could not expect to be included in an early exchange of men. He had to wait until his time in prison provided him enough seniority to place his name high on the exchange list before he could expect favorable results. Exchange offered the hope of eventual release, but it was always a time-consuming matter.

A parole for a military prisoner, if he was fortunate enough to obtain one, was not a complicated thing. Traditionally, a parole simply meant that a prisoner gave his word of honor, if he was released from captivity or given special privileges, to abide by the restrictions placed upon him by his captors; it was usually a promise to take no further part in the fighting until officially exchanged as a prisoner of war. A parole was an exciting possibility to a captive for many reasons. It depended upon the decision of a military commander, and such power could be exercised unilaterally. A parole could be granted without the protracted negotiations which always accompanied prisoner exchanges, and it was widely known among American captives that the British commanders made liberal use of paroles during the war.

The British employed paroles for American captives to solve a variety of problems. Basically, however, there were four goals for the British parole system to achieve. One of those goals was simply to return men, whom the British had no desire to detain, to their homes. At the beginning of the war this practice was common. Evidently the British authorities did not expect a lengthy conflict, and granting parole seemed the sagacious approach to coping with the heavy influx of captives. Allowing men to return to their homes accomplished a dual purpose. First of all, it reduced the demand for prison quarters and quickly solved the administrative problem of imprisoning colonials. Secondly, such a policy was calculated to create the impression of a forceful yet humane adversary. Examples of the parole policy can be found early in the war. On September 21, 1776, William Howe addressed a letter to George Washington and informed him that a group of paroled American prisoners had just arrived at New York from Quebec, and he would send them to Elizabethtown, New Jersey, so they could return to American lines.[20] As a result of this action, a total of 430 Americans, both officers and enlisted men, were allowed to return to American lines.[21] General Guy Carleton, who commanded British forces in Canada and had sent the 430 men to New York, paroled sixteen more Americans on October 10, 1776, on condition that they refrain from further military action until they were officially exchanged. Carleton also exacted the promise from the parolees that they would return to captivity at some future date if he summoned them.[22] As the war lengthened, the practice of paroling men just to allow them to return to their homes, for humane or propaganda purposes, became less frequent. Generals Howe and Carleton should be given their due. They did countenance such a program at the outset of the struggle.

A second aspect of the parole policy followed by the British Army was to permit American officers to be released from the prisons, but to require the parolees to remain within British lines. This program was principally utilized, on any scale, at New York City. Following the campaign of 1776-77, the prison compounds were critically overcrowded. General Howe, prompted by the teeming prisons, inaugurated the policy of allowing American officers to seek accommodations in New York City or on Long Island which, of course, were under the supervision of the British Army.[23] Many American officers located themselves as roomers and boarders in private homes as a result of General Howe's generous policy. This privilege was forthcoming for two basic reasons. One, already mentioned, was to reduce the overcrowded conditions of the prisons and to remove the officers from contact with their men, which might improve the British Army's control over the inmates. A second reason was to set an example of giving the American officers extra consideration, which might improve the conditions of British officers detained in American prisons. The policy of quartering paroled American officers at carefully selected sites, especially on Long Island, continued until the end of the war.[24] To a lesser extent, paroling officers to billets outside the regular prisons in such places as Philadelphia, Charleston, and elsewhere was allowed, but it was on a smaller scale than at New York City due to the shorter length of time those areas were occupied by British forces.

A third facet of the parole program was the release of large numbers of prisoners, both officers and enlisted men, who were granted permission to return to their homes to await exchange or an end to the war. Such a policy was seldom employed, but it was a part of the program. A good example of the wholesale paroling of American forces came with capitulation of Charleston, South Carolina, in 1780. The city of Charleston was heavily defended, and General Clinton's assault upon it yielded in excess of five thousand captives.[25] While the terms for the surrender of the city were under negotiation, Clinton recognized that he could not provide adequate facilities for so many captives. As a result, the articles of capitulation, under which General Benjamin Lincoln surrendered Charleston to Clinton, provided that all militia in the garrison were automatically paroled and granted permission to return to their homes.[26] The Continental forces were all imprisoned, but the militia were allowed parole. Literally hundreds of men were paroled with one stroke of the pen. This sort of parole, a blanket parole, was most uncommon. Clinton chose to use such an approach because it was practical, but he should be commended for his decision. Sir Henry must have realized that the overcrowded prisons caused a high death rate among the inmates, and for that reason he may have decided not to demand the incarceration of the entire Charleston garrison.

A fourth and final reason for issuing paroles to American personnel was to release men whose personal problems warranted special consideration. On a few occasions Americans were paroled and permitted to return to their homes due to declining health, illness of members of their family, family distress of one sort or another, or pressing problems which could not be dealt with while in prison.[27] This type of parole was not common. All in all, the British military authorities granted paroles for a great many men for a variety of reasons, but it should be noted that many petitions for paroles were never acted upon. Hundreds of Americans who sought release from prison via parole were disappointed by the refusal of their entreaties to be set free.

The document which admitted the prisoner to parole was standard in its features. A parole defined the terms under which the captive was released. Hundreds of the paroles were written, and the language of them varied little. A good example of such a document is one issued to Captain John Postell at Charleston on May 19, 1780. It reads:

> I do hereby acknowledge myself a prisoner of war on my parole, to His Excellency Sir Henry Clinton, and that I am thereby engaged until I am exchanged or otherwise released therefrom, to remain at my plantation in the Parish of St. Marks, in the county of Craven, in the province of South Carolina. And that I shall not in the meantime, do or cause anything to be done prejudicial to the success of his Majesty's arms, or have intercourse or hold correspondence with his enemies, and that upon a summons from his Excellency, or other person having authority thereto, that I will surrender myself to him or them at such time and place as I shall be hereafter required. Witness my hand this 19th day of May, 1780 – Jno. Postell, Lieut. Adj't, Craven county. Witnesses – John Gillon, McKillop, Major Stewart, Commissary prisoners, John Hamilton. A true copy taken from the original in my office, this 12th of May 1781.[28]

Captain Postell and many other Americans gained release from prison by such an instrument which, while placing several restrictions upon them, spared them the hazards of languishing in prison awaiting an exchange of prisoners.

Granting paroles to prisoners of war raised another troublesome issue between the British and American armed forces. A good many American parolees failed to conform to the requirements of their paroles, and a healthy correspondence materialized regarding the recall of parole violators during the war. Men who were recalled by the British were usually returned to prison for one of two reasons.

The most common cause for revocation of a parole was the escape of a prisoner after he had been paroled with the stipulation to stay in a specified area within the British lines. The cynical use of a parole as the first step toward an escape began early in the war. Several American officers carried off a successful escape from the New York vicinity in early 1777, after having been paroled by General Howe, and returned to American lines. They claimed they were compelled to violate their paroles because they were not properly supplied with food, clothing, and other necessary items. When the matter was brought to General Washington's attention he personally investigated the matter, and he concluded that the officers were telling the truth, but he ordered them to return to New York City.[29] Washington was sympathetic to the plight of his officers, but he was afraid their illegal action might endanger the hopes of other men to gain parole.[30]

British complaints of Americans violating their paroles by escaping were numerous during the Revolution. On December 12, 1778, Joshua Loring addressed a letter to John Beatty containing the names of eighty Americans who had broken their paroles and demanded that they be returned to New York City at once.[31] The following year, at the request of General Washington, Beatty composed a list of names totalling ninety-eight who had violated their paroles.[32] General Washington consistently had such issues and claims investigated and ordered those guilty of reneging on their parole agreements to return to British lines.[33] In fact, Washington labored to maintain as much justice regarding the runaway parolees as was humanly possible. He instructed John Beatty to inform the British that every effort would be made to restore all the missing men, but if they could not be located then Washington would parole enough British officers to make up the deficit and send them to New York.[34] General Washington viewed the whole process of parole with a keen interest, and he endeavored to keep the system as equitable as possible. The British authorities were equally concerned with maintaining the parole program, and they cast a rather tolerant eye on the escapes of men who pledged to cooperate with their captors.

The second major cause for withdrawal of paroles from American personnel came through misinterpretation of the terms of the agreement. Many Americans simply failed to comprehend fully their obligations and inadvertently erred in their conduct. Cases of this sort were also dealt with firmly by the British. Their position was clear and justifiable concerning innocent violation of a parole. No matter how well intentioned the parolee might be, he had to be punished for breaking his parole, since too lenient an attitude on the part of the British might lead to the complete breakdown of the system in general. The punishment usually was the temporary loss of parole and a brief confinement in the Provost.[35] The parole system depended heavily upon the parolee's pledging his honor to live up to the terms of his agreement and his being cognizant of his responsibilities as well as of his privileges. The vast majority of the parolees did behave honorably.

Occasionally serious misunderstanding arose between the British military authorities and American parolees. Perhaps the most tragic case of parole misunderstanding arose in South Carolina in 1780-81. It involved a militia officer named Isaac Hayne and demonstrated how high the price could be for ignorance or misinformation.

Isaac Hayne's military career in the Revolution commenced in his native South Carolina when he was commissioned a Captain in the Colleton County Regiment of Foot in 1775.[36] His military record was one of intermittent and inconspicuous service until 1780. Hayne was one of the Patriots who rallied to the futile defense of Charleston in 1780. When he arrived in Charleston to lend his strength to its defense, he enlisted in a militia regiment as a private. Hayne was elevated to the rank of colonel, but he soon resigned his commission after being disillusioned by several quarrels among his fellow officers and returned to the ranks as a private.[37] Hayne took an active part in the abortive defense of Charleston against the British onslaught of 1780, and he was taken prisoner when the city capitulated to Clinton. General Clinton, as mentioned earlier, paroled all the militia captured with the fall of Charleston, and Isaac Hayne was among those men admitted to parole. He returned to his home and remained neutral in his conduct as required by his parole.[38] Until the summer of 1781, Hayne's circumstances were similar to those of hundreds of other men in South Carolina. In the summer of 1781, however, he was summoned to Charleston and told that he must declare himself a British subject and sign an oath of allegiance or submit to close confinement.[39] Hayne was not alone; many of the paroled militia were faced with the same choice.

After pondering the issue carefully, Hayne decided to sign the oath of allegiance since it was the only way, distasteful as it was, that he could return to his family. An epidemic of smallpox had begun to ravage his home area, and it threatened his family.[40] When he read the oath of allegiance prior to signing it he noticed a clause which obliged him to "with his arms support royal government."[41] He objected to the clause. He was assured, however, by General James Paterson, Commandant of Charleston, that he would never be called upon to fulfill that part of the oath.[42] Hayne accepted Paterson's verbal assurance at face value, signed the oath, and hastened back to his family.

Not long after signing the oath of allegiance, Hayne was called upon to take up arms and support the British in the struggle against Nathanael Greene's forces in South Carolina.[43] At this point, Hayne made a fateful decision. He decided the British had first violated the terms of his original parole, then they had violated the verbal agreement of his oath of loyalty,[44] and that now he was a man free to act as he chose. Hayne believed that the British had acted illegally in both situations, and now they had nullified all contracts, written or verbal. He rejoined the American military forces and began to raise a regiment. Colonel Hayne became quite active in the campaign of 1781. On July 8, 1781, he was captured at Horseshoe, South Carolina, and taken to Charleston and imprisoned.[45]

Upon his arrival in Charleston as a prisoner, Colonel Hayne's legal status was surrounded by confusion. Should he be treated as a British subject guilty of treason or was he simply a parole violator accused of a serious breach of his agreement? Regardless of which viewpoint prevailed, Hayne was vulnerable to reprisal. The British charged that he was guilty of what amounted to treason and sought to make an example of him. Colonel Hayne argued that the British had broken their contract with him by calling him to military service, and that he had acted legally. After some complicated legal proceedings, Hayne was condemned to die by hanging. He was executed on August 4, 1781, at Charleston, South Carolina.[46]

A storm of protest arose over Hayne's execution, and a strong demand for retaliation was voiced by numerous Patriots from many quarters.[47] Fortunately for many innocent men, the demands for retaliation were ignored and the tragedy was not compounded. Nevertheless, the Hayne episode reflected how complicated something as simple as a parole could become. Few men came close to Colonel Hayne's predicament during the war.

Most American prisoners of war, if they were realistic, understood that an exchange of captives was their only certain path to gain their unconditional release from prison. Without question more Americans returned from enemy prisons through the process of exchange than by all the other means of liberation combined. Under ordinary circumstances, exchanging prisoners of war is not an unduly complex issue between belligerent nations. Negotiations, often lengthy and complicated in nature, have to be conducted to arrange the details of how, when, and where captives will be delivered. Lists of prisoners have to be compiled to provide for an accurate accounting of personnel, and a myriad of details require attention. Normally the complications are temporary in character, and the delays are motivated by concern for the welfare of the men about to be repatriated. When sovereign nations make war the issues surrounding the exchange of prisoners, in a legal sense, are not complicated. All that is necessary is for the warring nations to agree to exchange captives on terms they deem favorable or useful. No one can argue the legality or probity of one sovereign nation's entering into an agreement with another sovereign nation to recover its captured citizens. Unfortunately, however, not all the conflicts of men conform to the precise legal or diplomatic standards which apply to international war. Special circumstances can escalate a delicate problem into a nearly insoluble issue. In the case of undeclared wars, civil wars, or colonial rebellions the handicaps to smooth exchange of prisoners are manifold. Since the American Revolution was viewed as a colonial rebellion by Great Britain, certain difficulties in exchanging captives were inherent.

The exchange of prisoners of war was an extremely sensitive issue for Great Britain during the American Revolution. In the official view of the British government, the American captives were rebels, yet it never seriously contemplated treating them as such. If American soldiers and sailors had been disposed of as rebels, it would have created an ugly and bloody crisis. The British nation was too civilized for that to occur.

The British government persisted in defining American captives as rebels for three reasons. First of all, the American captives were, in fact, rebels; no other viewpoint was politically acceptable even though the men were not meted out the punishment reserved for traitors. Secondly, by officially terming the captives as rebels, European nations were served notice that the struggle in North America was a family affair, and one in which they should refrain from involving themselves. Finally, by declaring the captives as rebels, the government avoided the need to negotiate formally with the Revolutionary governments for the exchange of prisoners. Such agreements are concluded between sovereign nations, and, in the view of the British government, the colonies had no claim to sovereignty. Thus Great Britain could manage to avoid a tacit recognition of American independence which, of course, was one of her primary goals in the struggle. Instead, the military commanders were empowered to arrange for partial exchanges of prisoners as their wisdom and needs might dictate. From the government's standpoint, allowing the commanders discretionary powers regarding exchange was best of all possible answers. Both political and humane instincts could be served at the same time.

Thus the British policy controlling the exchange of captives emerged. American captives were classified as rebels for political and diplomatic reasons, but they were not to be punished as rebels. Exchanges were to be negotiated by the British military commanders in whatever fashion they deemed proper. The negotiations which preceeded an exchange were to be conducted in a manner which pledged the honor of the commander, and not the government, that the bargain would be consumated. Until the end of the war, the exchanges were partial in character, and they were, in effect, a series of gentlemen's agreements which were never elevated to the status of a treaty.

Congress began its quest to establish a set of rules governing prisoner exchanges on December 2, 1775. On that day, Congress took its first exploratory step in quest of an exchange agreement with Great Britain. Congress had no precedent to direct its action and little experience with the issue of exchange of captives. Nevertheless, Congress boldly declared the principles which were to be followed in prisoner of war exchanges. It resolved that prisoners of war were to be exchanged ". . . citizen for citizen, officer for officer of equal rank and soldier for soldier."[48] No mention of naval personnel was made in the original resolution attempting to define congressional rules governing exchange. This oversight was corrected on July 26, 1776, when Congress reiterated the statement of the previous

December and included the clause that naval personnel were to be exchanged sailor for sailor.[49] As soon as Congress took this first tentative step to try to open the door to a prisoner exchange, General Washington commenced a correspondence with General Howe seeking to arrange repatriation of captives on terms consistent with the regulations laid down by Congress.[50] Washington's efforts proved fruitless in early 1776. Not many captives were detained by either side at that point, and the British were not overly concerned about exchanging the few they held. The first American overtures for an exchange were largely ignored.

Even though no real progress toward an agreement on an exchange policy was evident in early 1776, Congress continued to evaluate the situation and to issue additional regulations. On May 16, 1776, for example, Congress declared that enemy prisoners taken by Continental armed forces were not to be exchanged under any authority except that of the Continental Congress.[51] Through this action Congress hoped to create the notion that it was the focal point for all decisions relating to prisoner exchange. The logical beginning point was for Congress to claim authority for the exchange of all prisoners captured by its forces, and, in the process, to develop an expertise on the matter which would train the states to look to it for leadership when the time for exchanges arose. It did not take long for the Congress to seek to assert its hegemony on the issue. On July 22, 1776, Congress passed another important milestone relevant to exchange of captives. It decided to delegate authority to its military commanders in each department to negotiate the prisoner exchanges on the basis of officer for officer of equal rank in either the land or sea service, sailor for sailor, soldier for soldier, and citizen for citizen.[52] In the first few months of the war, Congress pursued a dual purpose of trying, on the one hand, to accumulate authority governing all prisoner exchanges, and, on the other hand, of delegating responsibility for effecting such exchanges to its military commanders. Ultimately, Congress succeeded.

Armed with a mandate from Congress, General Washington renewed his efforts to seek an agreement with Howe to facilitate an exchange of captives. A flurry of letters passed between the commanders, which proved productive. Howe agreed to a partial exchange if each commander could choose by name the men he wished to recover.[53] Washington transmitted Howe's proposal to Congress for ratification and received its approval on August 27, 1776.[54]

On September 21, 1776, Howe sent General Washington a list of the men he was to produce, and the first significant exchange was set in motion.[55] General Washington busied himself with the task of gathering the designated cartel of prisoners, and the exchange began.[56] On September 25, 1776, Howe reported to Lord George Germain that an exchange was underway which had caused several British and American officers to be repatriated.[57] General Washington also composed a list of the men he wished to recover in the cartel, but he was disappointed to discover that his wishes were not always fulfilled. He often got men returned whom the British chose to send and not the captives he had specified.[58]

The program of repatriation did not function smoothly, but it was a beginning which held some promise for the future. As the first exchange took place, two mildly distressing facts became apparent to Washington. When discussing exchange of captives, the British would consider only a partial exchange consisting of specified individuals. A general exchange of captives was never offered. And, when agreements were reached permitting partial exchanges, the agreements were nothing more than a document predicated upon Howe's word and honor. Howe was an honorable man, but Congress sought a long term, formal commitment. No permanent arrangement for the repatriation of American captives was ever seriously considered by General Howe or his staff. Congress, therefore, had to content itself with what it could obtain, but partial exchanges fell somewhat short of its hopes.

There are no available statistics which indicate how many men were involved in the partial exchange in the latter part of 1776. Generals Howe and Washington each found reasons for dissatisfaction with the interchange of prisoners, but they desired to continue the repatriation program. In January of 1777, General Howe proceeded with preparations to carry out additional exchanges by instructing Lieutenant Colonel William Wolcott to familiarize himself with the techniques and regulations surrounding the topic and to stand ready to meet with an American representative to work out the details of another cartel.[59] General Howe soon received notification that American authorities were anxious to discuss another exchange.[60] While their willingness to negotiate was apparent, Howe was not informed that the Americans would have some new demands to make at the proposed talks.[61]

In early March, when Lieutenant Colonel Wolcott and Lieutenant Colonel Robert H. Harrison, his American counterpart, met at Brunswick, New Jersey, the talks soon broke down due in large part to American demands.[62] The meeting between Wolcott and Harrison stalled because of failure to reach accord on two points raised by Harrison. Harrison, as he was instructed to do, called for a regular exchange system to be established, and asked that General Charles Lee, who had been captured in 1776, be declared a prisoner of war and eligible for exchange.[63] General Lee, a former British Army officer, had been captured in New Jersey, and he had not been listed as a prisoner of war. Washington fully understood that the hopes of establishing a general exchange at this meeting were slight, but he was deeply concerned about the welfare of Lee. Harrison was ordered not to yield on the point involving Lee. He did not, and the meeting was soon dissolved. Congress readily supported Washington's demand that General Lee be classified a prisoner of war entitled to exchange. On May 24, 1777, Congress resolved that when Lee was designated as a prisoner of war by his captors then General Washington was free to renew prisoner exchanges.[64]

Washington wrote Congress and gratefully acknowledged its support, and, in the same letter, he voiced a new concern. He stated his suspicion that the British were purposefully repatriating men whose health had begun to decline while holding back healthier captives.[65] Another quarrel loomed which future meetings would have to discuss.

The deadlock concerning further exchanges continued into the summer of 1777. Congress approved of Washington's conduct, and voted to empower him to negotiate an exchange ". . . in such manner, and on such terms, as he shall judge expedient."[66] Washington never wavered from his demand that General Lee be awarded the status of a prisoner of war even though it brought exchanges to a halt.[67] Finally, Lord George Germain solved the impasse by instructing General Howe to offer Lee for exchange whenever he thought the propitious moment arrived.[68] So, by the end of 1777, only sporadic partial exchanges had been conducted. Several questions also emerged during 1777. The demand for a regular exchange system had become much stronger, and the Americans had begun to complain about the alleged practice of returning captives who were ill before healthy men were allowed exchange. All in all, 1777 was a year of frustration for both Washington and Howe.

The controversy attending the exchange of prisoners of war did not lessen in 1778. A series of events served to tinge the question with more urgency and uncertainty. One of the events was the surrender of General John Burgoyne and his army to the triumphant American forces at Saratoga, New York, in October of 1777. Such a large bag of prisoners finally gave American negotiators a stronger bargaining position when the time for the renewal of exchange talks came. There also was a change in the British high command in 1778. General Howe vacated the post of Commander in Chief in 1778, and General Henry Clinton was appointed to succeed him.

The British Army's change in command strengthened American resolve to seek a formal exchange agreement based on something other than a military man's word of honor. Clinton was an honorable man, but the sudden shift in personnel in the high command demonstrated the danger in negotiating an exchange with an officer who might not be in a position of authority when the time came for the bargain to be completed. And finally, the impact of the alliance concluded between the United States and France influenced the exchange question. With the entry of France into the conflict, the British could no longer expect a quick end to the war. Since the war appeared destined to prolongation, the need for more rapid and large scale exchange seemed more essential.

One of the more promising omens, in early 1778, was Howe's decision to permit General Lee's name to be posted as a prisoner of war. As soon as Lee's name appeared on the prisoner of war lists, Washington moved to arrange his return to American lines.[69] The announcement that Lee was available for exchange produced two good results. General Lee got his freedom; he was exchanged on May 6, 1778.[70] Additionally, the tension between Washington and his British counterpart was partially relieved, which permitted useful communication regarding prisoner exchange to be renewed. General Washington was pleased with the results of his demand for Lee's return. He stood firm, and he got what he wanted.

Shortly after learning that Lee was eligible for exchange, Washington planned to reopen talks to bring about a general exchange of captives. He summoned Elias Boudinot to his headquarters, and they conferred on strategy.[71] Washington then secured Howe's consent to convene a conference of officers to consider the possibility of such an agreement. By early March, it had been arranged that selected British and American officers would meet in Germantown, Pennsylvania, to discuss matters which would lead to a general exchange of captives.[72] Howe appointed Colonels Charles O'Hara and Humphrey Stephens and Captain Richard Fitzpatrick to represent him.[73] Washington selected Colonel William Grayson and Lieutenant Colonels Robert H. Harrison, Alexander Hamilton, and Elias Boudinot to meet with the team of British officers.[74] On March 31, 1778, the deputies of the two commanders met in Germantown to thresh out the details of a general exchange.[75] The Germantown meeting quickly foundered. The American delegates insisted that the British officers were not armed with sufficient authority for a general exchange. They claimed that General Howe's word was not an adequate basis for such an arrangement.[76] O'Hara, Stephens, and Fitzpatrick had no instructions on this issue, so the session was soon terminated.

General Washington was disappointed with the outcome of the Germantown meeting; he contacted Howe and suggested another session. Howe promptly assented to the proposal, and another meeting was scheduled at Newtown, Pennsylvania.[77] On April 10-11, 1778, the second round of talks commenced and deadlocked on the same issue as had the German-town meeting.[78] The Americans persisted in their assertion that Howe's personal word was not sufficient basis for such an important agreement.[79] The British negotiators offered only Howe's authority for a general exchange, and so the Americans withdrew from the talks.[80] The American campaign for a formal treaty to permit the general exchange of captives had begun inauspiciously.

While there was no progress in settling upon an agreement for a general repatriation of captives, there were several partial exchanges transacted in 1778.[81] A partial exchange proved to be a relatively easy matter to conduct. Most of the exchanges of this sort were arranged by the British and American Commissary Generals with only a minimum of supervision by their superiors. Partial exchanges were made upon the authority of the two commanders, and, therefore, were in no way prejudicial to Great Britain's steadfast decision of refusing to negotiate officially with the Americans.

In a letter to Washington dated November 10, 1778, General Clinton, who was now the British Commander in Chief, suggested another conference of specially delegated officers to negotiate a partial exchange of captives.[82] Numerous American officers were still prisoners of war, and Clinton was interested in exchanging them for the men of General Burgoyne's army who had surrendered at Saratoga the previous year. He had offered earlier to exchange American officers by composition, which simply meant that he would accept several men of inferior rank for one man of superior rank, and he had been rebuffed.[83] Now he proposed a meeting at Amboy, New Jersey, in December to explore the possibility of a rather special partial exchange. Washington queried Congress about the offer, and it responded that he should look into the matter and send officers to Amboy.[84] As soon as Congress gave its consent, Washington notified Clinton that he would send Lieutenant Colonels Alexander Hamilton and Robert H. Harrison to Amboy for a conference on December 12, 1778.[85] Clinton chose Colonels West Hyde and Charles O'Hara to present his views, and the meeting was set.[86]

The Amboy conference met and ended on December 12, 1778.[87] Hamilton and Harrison proposed that officers of equal rank be exchanged, and if any American officers were left in prison after such an exchange, then British privates would be used to redeem the remaining Americans.[88] Hyde and O'Hara sought to begin an exchange by composition at the outset. A deadlock was the result. Hamilton and Harrison thought Clinton's motive was the recovery of sorely needed manpower while giving up a handful of American officers.[89] Another year of frustration was recorded in 1778.

Partial exchanges were, however, effected on a fairly regular basis in

1779.[90] Congress chose, on March 6, 1779, to increase the powers of General Washington to exchange captives. Washington was authorized to negotiate general or partial exchanges, and he was granted the right to employ the principle of composition in a partial exchange if he chose to do so.[91] This marked the first time that Congress publicly expressed any view on exchange by composition.

A week after Congress altered its position on exchange, Washington contacted Clinton and suggested another meeting at Amboy, New Jersey, to attempt to establish a general cartel of captives.[92] Clinton responded and indicated his willingness to arrange yet another meeting on the issue of a general exchange.[93] On April 12, 1779, the American Colonels William Davies and Robert H. Harrison met with Colonels West Hyde and John André at Amboy to debate the details of an exchange.[94] Again, the face-to-face approach produced nothing. The conference finally dissolved upon the request of the Americans. Hyde and André reported to Clinton that they believed the Americans had only two goals for attending the meeting: first, to silence the clamor of American prisoners demanding that they be exchanged by meeting with the British and then blaming them for the breakdown in the negotiations; and, secondly, to try to draw the British into a recognition of American independence by the creation of a regular cartel backed by the weight of the British government.[95] All of the several special conferences so far had produced no important results whatever.

During these years of one unproductive conference after another, partial exchanges were continued with minimum difficulty, but Washington was not satisfied.[96] He desired to establish a formal agreement which would permit his subordinates to exchange prisoners completely, and one that would automatically provide for repatriation of captives without controversy in the future. His goal was an admirable but elusive one. Congress shared Washington's ambition and authorized him to try again to gain such an agreement.[97]

On February 29, 1780, Washington addressed a letter to Baron von Knyphausen, one of General Clinton's staff officers, and proposed another session of talks between American and British representatives at Amboy, New Jersey, on March 9, 1780.[98] Washington briefly recapitulated the series of failures to reach accord on the exchange question, and he asserted his belief that the time had arrived for definitive action on the matter. Washington's letter received prompt and encouraging attention, so he dispatched General Arthur St. Clair and Lieutenant Colonels Edward Carrington and Alexander Hamilton to meet with a British delegation composed of General William Phillips and Lieutenant Colonels Cosmo Gordon and Chapel Norton.[99]

The third Amboy conference finally convened on March 10 and lasted through March 14, 1780.[100] Basically, the commissioners were to debate the issue of a general exchange which would end a question of three years' duration. They were, however, to look into any other matter regarding prisoners of war they might choose to discuss. As usual, however, the American representatives opened the meeting by asking upon what authority the British proposed a general cartel be established. The reply, as usual, was that General Clinton offered his personal assurances that any agreement would be honored, but that the government refused to elevate such a commitment to the status of a treaty. Upon this declaration, the Americans reiterated their long-standing contention that they doubted the wisdom of such an arrangement.[101] The British officers were not surprised by the response, and, after four more days of pointless harangue, the meeting adjourned. Nothing was accomplished.

Again, after failing to establish a general cartel, Washington and Clinton relied upon their respective Commissary Generals of captives, Abraham Skinner and Joshua Loring, to carry out partial exchanges to repatriate prisoners. A lively correspondence developed among the four men, and details leading to several small exchanges of captives were settled.[102] On November 7, 1780, for example, Washington reported to the Continental Congress that he had recently entered into an agreement for the exchange which released 140 officers and 476 privates from the prisons in New York.[103] General Nathanael Greene, Commander of the Southern Department, was empowered to exchange prisoners in South Carolina, and he managed to liberate a few men.[104] For five years, partial exchange proved the only means to recover captured personnel.

After the many failures to reach an agreement on a general exchange, Washington and Clinton did not seriously reopen the question in 1781. Instead, the commanders contented themselves with the system of exchange as it had developed through practice during the war. General Greene's staff became more active in 1781, and several partial exchanges were concluded in South Carolina.[105] Basically, in regard to the prisoner of war issue, the year of 1781 was uneventful. There were few important partial exchanges of captives and no significant alteration in policy.

In a few rare instances American prisoners of war were exchanged for British captives outside of North America. Scores of crewmen from American vessels were imprisoned in several prisons in Great Britain. These men had little hope of returning to America until after the war ended and all prisoners were released. Once American naval personnel were delivered to such prisons as Forton or Mill, they usually expected to sit out the war there. Not many Americans were transported from England to New York and offered for exchange. So, once seamen were detained in Great Britain, their chance for an early release diminished; the majority of American captives unlucky enough to find themselves in prisons in Great Britain were there for the duration of the war.

A handful of Americans incarcerated in Great Britain were, however, exchanged. In May of 1778, Benjamin Franklin, who was stationed on diplomatic duty in Paris, initiated contact with the British government and offered to trade prisoners.[106] He informed the British government that he had nearly two hundred captives in his custody, and he offered to exchange them for an equal number of American seamen.[107] Franklin received assurance, in early June of 1778, that an informal agreement could be made and the exchange transacted.[108] Franklin and his diplomatic colleagues, Arthur Lee and John Adams, then proceeded to negotiate with the British government through David Hartley, a member of Parliament, who served as the intermediary.

The American diplomats requested that seamen who had been confined the longest be exchanged first, and they promised to return British captives in similar fashion.[109] The American diplomats further declared that they were willing to accept custody of all Americans detained in Great Britain and promised that any balance of captives due Great Britain after the exchange would be made up in America.[110] The second part of the offer was politely declined, but the British agreed to an exchange of equal numbers of captives. A host of minor details were ironed out, and, finally, on September 9, 1778, the French government granted permission for British vessels to disembark American captives at the ports of L'Orient and Nantes.[111] The first contingent of American captives left England for exchange in France in February of 1779.[112] Another small group of prisoners arrived in France during July of 1779, and they were exchanged.[113] And at least one more cartel of prisoners, numbering 119 men, was exchanged in France in 1779.[114]

Franklin and his comrades enjoyed only limited success in bargaining for the release of Americans via exchange. They never had many British captives to offer in exchanges which, of course, restricted their activities. There were plenty of British captives in America, but it proved impossible for Franklin to persuade the British government to send him captives and receive compensation for them in America. Moreover, the British government was hesitant to continue the negotiations with Franklin for fear of lending credence to the American claims of independence. The only prisoner exchanges, of any consequence, outside North America were the ones arranged in 1779 by Franklin and his cohorts.

At the end of 1781, the practice of exchanging captives by composition commenced.[115] Exchanging a man of superior rank for several men of inferior rank had been considered as early as 1779, but no action was forthcoming on this concept at that time.[116] In March of 1780, at one of the Amboy conferences, a schedule for exchanging by composition was discussed which finally became the basis for such a practice.[117] It established the following ratio for exchanging by composition.

Lieutenant General	1,044
Major General	372
Brigadier General	200
Colonel	100
Lieutenant Colonel	72
Major	28
Captain	16
1st Lieutenant	8
2nd Lieutenant, Ensign	4
Sergeant	2
Corporal, Drummer, Fifer, Private, and Volunteer	1
Adjutant, Quartermaster of Regiment and Corps	6
Surgeon to Regiment and Corps	6
Mates to Regiment and Corps	4

When Lord Cornwallis was captured he held the rank of Lieutenant General. Using the composition method, he could be exchanged by meeting the value of his rank, which was 1,044. Cornwallis could be redeemed by an exchange of 1,044 American privates or combinations of the various ranks. For example, nine colonels (9 x 100 = 900) plus two Lieutenant Colonels (2 x 72 = 144) would equal the necessary tariff of 1,044. A Colonel could be exchanged for a Lieutenant Colonel (72) and a Major (28) which would equal the figure of one hundred which was the worth of a Colonel according to the tariff system. The main reason for the composition means was to provide some easy way to exchange high ranking officers. In an exchange of officer for officer of equal rank, a Lieutenant General might have to wait for years before the enemy captured an officer of equal rank. Such exchanges were infrequently proposed,[118] but they did occur.

The early part of 1782 was somewhat paradoxical. The defeat at Yorktown yielded many new and important prisoners to American armed forces. As the year began there were the usual communications regarding partial exchanges, treatment of captives, and other matters passing between American and British authorities.[119] On the surface everything appeared to be as it had been for the previous six years. Yet there was an undercurrent which indicated that there was a growing belief that the war was about to end. On March 25, 1782, six months after the capture of Lord Cornwallis and his entire army at Yorktown, Parliament passed an act which legally defined American captives as prisoners of war.[120] In doing so Parliament removed all legal barriers to open and final negotiations for the repatriation of all captives, and, of course, extended tacit recognition of American independence several months prior to the Treaty of Paris of 1783.

General Guy Carleton, the new Commander in Chief who replaced Clinton in 1782, presided over the final stages of exchanging American captives as the war drew to a conclusion. Carleton offered to discuss the details of final exchange in the summer of 1782.[121] It was September, however, before negotiations could be arranged; on September 23, 1782, Generals William Heath and Henry Knox met with Carleton's representatives at Tappan, New York. General Washington hoped that Heath and Knox would conclude the long awaited agreement which would permit a total exchange of men, but the Tappan meeting failed to produce it. [122] Partial exchanges, of a broader scope than ever before, were continued. All the remaining obstacles to final repatriation were finally surmounted early in 1783.

One of the most heartening signs witnessed in 1782 was the arrival of several British transports carrying American seamen who had been imprisoned in Great Britain. By August 19, 1782, the sloop *Adventure* was anchored in Boston harbor awaiting official instructions from General Carleton as to when the four hundred American captives aboard should be released.[123] Three days later the *Adamant* arrived at Boston carrying 115 prisoners.[124] Three cartel vessels, as they were termed, bearing a total of 701 captives arrived at Boston during August of 1782.[125] At the same time, a vessel named *Tyger* arrived on August 20, 1782 at Philadelphia with 132 prisoners.[126] The 833 returning Americans aboard the cartel ships were from Forton and Mill prisons and other prison sites in Great Britain. The captives were transported to America by order of the British government without any consultation with the American government. Great Britain had begun to return the men without any request to do so, and this prompt and unilateral action was certainly welcome. Most of these vessels had departed from Great Britain in June, which was only two months after the Parliament had awarded prisoner of war status to all American captives. The details of the last exchange of captives in North America were still a bit clouded with minor controversy, but Great Britain's intent was clear. The war was finished.

The final exchange of prisoners of war was concluded in 1783. Washington happily recorded that the British had withdrawn from Charleston,

South Carolina, in January of 1783, and he noted that General Greene had recovered all the prisoners detained in that area.[127] A general exchange was a little slower in materializing in the north. New York City was the last stronghold of the British Army in the United States of America which meant, of course, that the final chapter to the story was written there. One of the last problems obstructing the completion of the interchange of captives was the settlement of accounts for the expenditure of money in caring for prisoners.[128] This issue and several other lesser ones were solved by a meeting between Washington and General Carleton at Tappan, New York, on May 6, 1783.[129] By July 1, 1783, Washington reported to Benjamin Lincoln, the Secretary at War, that the general exchange of prisoners was finished except for a few German mercenaries who were about to be liberated.[130] Later that month, Benjamin Franklin recorded that all Americans once detained in Great Britain had been set at liberty.[131] After slightly more than eight years, all the American captives were free at last.

FOOTNOTES

[1] There are no reliable statistics regarding escaped prisoners.

[2] Peckham, *Memoirs of Adlum*, viii.

[3] *Ibid.*, 86.

[4] Dandridge, *American Prisoners*, 498.

[5] Bushnell, *Narrative of Hanford*, 160.

[6] George Washington to William Howe, January 13, 1777, Fitzpatrick, *Writings of Washington*, VII, 3.

[7] *Ibid.* Thatcher, *Journal*, 91. George Washington to William Howe, November 14, 1777, Fitzpatrick, *Writings of Washington*, X, 64-66.

[8] George Washington to President of Congress, March 12, 1778, *ibid.*, XI, 73.

[9] The Committee of Arrangement to George Washington, September 30, 1778, Burnett, *Letters*, III, 431-32.

[10] Lord George Germain to Sir Henry Clinton, November 9, 1780, Fitzpatrick, *Writings of Washington*, XV, 9n. Lord George Germain to Earl of Cornwallis, November 9, 1780, Charles Ross, ed., *Correspondence of Charles, First Marquis Cornwallis* (London, 1859), I, 80. Cited hereafter as Ross, *Correspondence of Cornwallis.*

[11] *Ibid.*

[12] Benjamin Lincoln to George Washington, September 25, 1780,

Sparks, *Correspondence*, III, 97. The terrible prison conditions are described in a letter from Peter Fayssoux to Dr. D. Ramsay, March 26, 1785, Gibbes, *Documentary History*, 117-21.

[13] John Mathews to Nathanael Greene, April 30, 1781, and John Mathews to George Washington, May 2, 1781, Burnett, *Letters*, VI, 72, 77.

[14] Report Based on Letters of General Moultrie, JCC, XX, 621. The Board of War to George Washington, June 22 1781, Burnett, *Letters,* VI, 125-26.

[15] Report of Committee for Considering the State of Prisoners in the hands of the Enemy, August 3, 1781, PCC, Roll 35, Item 128, 49-51.

[16] *Ibid.*

[17] *Ibid.*

[18] John Jay to Benjamin Franklin, July 9, 1781, Johnston, *Correspondence of Jay*, II, 52.

[19] PCC, Roll 35, Item 128, 71-73. For a brief account of British policy on enlisting American seamen detained in Great Britain see Prelinger, "Benjamin Franklin," 275.

[20] William Howe to George Washington, September 21, 1776, Washington Papers. Also see Sparks, *Correspondence*, I, 290.

[21] Return of Prisoners sent by General Guy Carleton from Canada to New York, September 21, 1776, Washington Papers.

[22] Force, *American Archives*, II, 1304.

[23] Sabine, *Diary of Fitch*, 105n. Peckham, *Memoirs of Adlum*, 89-91. Worthington C. Ford, ed., "British and American Prisoners of War, 1778," *The Pennsylvania Magazine of History and Biography*, XVII (1893), 161-74.

[24] Abraham Skinner to George Washington, November 3, 1780, Washington Papers. David Sproat to Abraham Skinner, January 29, 1781, Banks, *Sproat*, 44. List of American Colonels Prisoner to the British on Parole — New York, January 4, 1782, Washington Papers.

[25] Christopher Ward sets the number at 5,446. Christopher Ward, *The War of the Revolution*, edited by John Richard Alden (New York, 1952), II, 703.

[26] Tarleton, *History of the Campaign in the Southern Provinces*, 63. Henry Lee, *Memoirs of the War in the Southern Department of the United States*, edited by Robert E. Lee (New York, 1869), 449. Cited hereafter as Lee, *Memoirs.*

[27] Mathew Knox to Elias Boudinot, May 6, 1778, Thomas Luckett to Elias Boudinot, May 6, 1778, and Andrew Galbraith to Elias Boudinot, May 6, 1778, Boudinot Papers. Caesar Rodney to Thomas Bradford, September 17, 1778, Ryder, *Letters to Rodney*, 282. Robert Magaw to

William Howe, December 8, 1776, BHQP, Reel 3, Document 341.

[28] Gibbes, *Documentary History*, 36.

[29] George Washington to Brigadier General Alexander McDougall, May 23, 1777, Fitzpatrick, *Writings of Washington*, VIII, 108.

[30] *Ibid.*

[31] Joshua Loring to John Beatty, December 12, 1778, PCC, Roll 91, Item 78, III, 279-80. Return of Rebel officers come in from parole since the summons, February 19, 1779, Clinton Papers.

[32] Return of Officers charged with having broken their Parole, July 10, 1779, Washington Papers.

[33] George Washington to John Beatty, August 8, 1779, Fitzpatrick, *Writings of Washington*, XVI, 130-31. George Washington to John Beatty, October 30, 1779, Washington Papers.

[34] George Washington to John Beatty, November 10, 1779, Fitzpatrick, *Writings of Washington*, XVII, 89-90.

[35] Return of officers broke Parole from Long Island, June 9, 1779, Clinton Papers.

[36] "Papers of the First Council of Safety of the Revolutionary Party in South Carolina, June-November, 1775," *The South Carolina Historical and Genealogical Magazine*, II (1901), 6.

[37] Lee, *Memoirs*, 449. Francis B. Heitman, *Historical Register of Officers of the Continental Army During the War of the Revolution* (Baltimore, 1967), 281. Cited hereafter as Heitman, *Historical Register*.

[38] John B. O. Landrum, *Colonial and Revolutionary History of Upper South Carolina* (Greenville, South Carolina, 1897), 104. Cited hereafter as Landrum, *History of Upper South Carolina*.

[39] Robert Goodwyn Rhett, *Charleston an Epic of Carolina* (Richmond, 1940), 141-42. David Ramsay, M.D., *Ramsay's History of South Carolina From Its First Settlement In 1670 To The Year 1808* (Newberry, South Carolina, 1858), I, 260. Cited hereafter as Ramsay, *History*.

[40] Lee, *Memoirs*, 449-51.

[41] Ramsay, *History*, 260.

[42] *Ibid.*

[43] *Ibid.*, 261.

[44] *Ibid.*, Lee, *Memoirs*, 452. Landrum, *History of Upper South Carolina*, 337.

[45] Heitman, *Historical Register*, 281.

[46] C. Fraser to Mr. Hayne, July 26, 1781, C. Fraser to Mr. Hayne, July 27, 1781, and C. Fraser to Mr. Hayne, July 29, 1781, Gibbes, *Documentary History*, 108, 109. *The Royal Gazette*, (South Carolina), August 8, 1781.

[47] Lee, *Memoirs*, 459-462. Report of Opinion of the Officers of the Virginia Line, August 17, 1781, and Colonel William Henderson to Major General Greene, August 25, 1781, Nathanael Greene Papers, Library of Congress, Washington, D. C.

[48] PCC, Roll 72, Item 59, I-II, 43.

[49] *Ibid.*, 45.

[50] George Washington to General Howe, January 30, 1776, BHQP, Reel 2A, Document 116. George Washington to Samuel MacKay, April 11, 1776, Fitzpatrick, *Writings of Washington*, IV, 475.

[51] JCC, IV, 362. PCC, Roll 72, Item 59, I-II, 45.

[52] *Ibid.*

[53] George Washington to President of Congress, August 5, 1776, Fitzpatrick, *Writings of Washington*, V, 370.

[54] JCC, V, 708-709. PCC, Roll 72, Item 59, I-II, 46.

[55] William Howe to George Washington, September 21, 1776, Force, *American Archives*, II, 437-38.

[56] George Washington to Governor Jonathan Trumbull, September 26, 1776, George Washington to Massachusetts Legislature, September 29, 1776, Fitzpatrick, *Writings of Washington,* VI, 122, 129-30.

[57] General Sir William Howe to Lord George Germain, September 25, 1776, Sackville-Germain Papers. Ambrose Serle to Earl of Dartmouth, November 7, 1776, Stevens, *Facsimiles*, XXIII, Document 2044, 1.

[58] George Washington to Sir William Howe, December 1, 1776, and George Washington to Massachusetts Legislature, December 21, 1776, Fitzpatrick, *Writings of Washington*, VI, 322-23, 414.

[59] William Howe to Lieutenant Colonel William Wolcott, January 26, 1777, BHQP, Reel 3, Document 388.

[60] John Sullivan to William Howe, February 8, 1777, *ibid.,* Document 403.

[61] George Washington to Lieutenant Colonel Robert H. Harrison, March 4, 1777, Harold C. Syrett and Jacob E. Cooke, eds., *The Papers of Alexander Hamilton* (New York, 1961–), I, 198-99. Cited hereafter as Syrett and Cooke, *Papers of Hamilton.*

[62] Lieutenant Colonel William Wolcott to William Howe, March 11, 1777, BHQP, Reel 3, Document 435.

[63] Alexander Hamilton to New York Committee of Correspondence, April 5, 1777, Syrett and Cooke, *Papers of Hamilton*, I, 222. PCC, Roll 72, Item 59, I-II, 48. Baron de Kalb to Comte de Broglie. April 10, 1777, Stevens, *Facsimiles*, VIII, Document 808, 3.

[64] JCC, VII, 197.

[65] George Washington to President of Congress, May 28, 1777, Fitzpat-

rick, *Writings of Washington*, VIII, 131-33. This issue was often raised in correspondence between British and American authorities. Washington did suspect that the British used the exchange system to rid the prison of ailing captives while ignoring many healthy men who were at the top of the exchange lists in seniority and eligible for repatriation.

[66] JCC, VIII, 621.

[67] George Washington to William Howe, September 5, 1777, BHQP, Reel 3, Document 667.

[68] George Germain to William Howe, September 9, 1777, *ibid.*, Document 661.

[69] George Washington to Major Jacob Morris, January 27, 1778, Fitzpatrick, *Writings of Washington*, X, 357-58.

[70] George Washington to Sir William Howe, May 9, 1778, Syrett and Cooke, *Papers of Hamilton*, I, 438. Lafayette, *Memoirs*, 48-49. Heitman, *Historical Register*, 345. Boudinot, *Journal*, 76-79.

[71] Alexander Hamilton to Elias Boudinot, February 9, 1778, Washington Papers.

[72] PCC, Roll 72, Item 59, I-II, 52.

[73] William Howe to George Washington, March 2, 1778, BHQP, Reel 3A, Document 972.

[74] George Washington to Colonel William Grayson and Lieutenant Colonels Robert H. Harrison, Alexander Hamilton, and Elias Boudinot, March 28, 1778, Washington Papers.

[75] Syrett and Cooke, *Papers of Hamilton*, I, 454.

[76] Colonel William Grayson and Lieutenant Colonels Robert H. Harrison, Alexander Hamilton, and Elias Boudinot to George Washington, April 4, 1778, Syrett and Cooke, *Papers of Hamilton*, I, 454-56.

[77] George Washington to Colonel William Grayson, and Lieutenant Colonels Robert H. Harrison, Alexander Hamilton, and Elias Boudinot, April 4, 1778, Washington Papers.

[78] Colonel William Grayson, and Lieutenant Colonels Robert H. Harrison, Alexander Hamilton, and Elias Boudinot to George Washington, April 15, 1778, Syrett and Cooke, *Papers of Hamilton*, I, 475-78.

[79] *Ibid.*

[80] John Henry, Jr. to Thomas Johnson, Jr., April 20, 1778, Burnett, *Letters*, III, 180.

[81] Elias Boudinot to George Washington, May 13, 1778, Sparks, *Correspondence*, II, 122-23. JCC, X, 266. Timothy Taylor to Elias Boudinot, May 7, 1778, Boudinot Papers. George Washington to Alexander Hamilton, June 4, 1778, Fitzpatrick, *Writings of Washington*, XII, 17. Joshua Loring to Alexander Hamilton, June 5, 1778, Syrett and Cooke, *Papers of*

Hamilton, I, 494-95. Joshua Loring to John Beatty, October 28, 1778, PCC, Roll 98, Item 78, XIV, 247-249. John Beatty to Lord Rawdon, November 27, 1778, Clinton Papers.

[82] Henry Clinton to George Washington, November 10, 1778, BHQP, Reel 5, Document 1548.

[83] *Ibid.*

[84] PCC, Roll 72, Item 59, I-II, 55.

[85] George Washington to Henry Clinton, November 27, 1778, BHQP, Reel 5, Document 1584.

[86] Henry Clinton to Colonel Charles O'Hara and Colonel West Hyde, December 7, 1778, Clinton Papers.

[87] Henry Clinton to Lord George Germain, December 16, 1778, *ibid.*

[88] Robert H. Harrison and Alexander Hamilton to Charles O'Hara and West Hyde, December 12, 1778, *ibid.*

[89] Lieutenant Colonels Robert H. Harrison and Alexander Hamilton to George Washington, December 15, 1778, Syrett and Cooke, *Papers of Hamilton*, I, 598-99.

[90] John Beatty to George Washington, January 3, 1779, Washington Papers. The Marine Committee to the Governor of Virginia, March 3, 1779, JCC, XIII, 110. Richard Henry Lee to Patrick Henry, March 3, 1779, James Curtis Ballagh, ed., *The Letters of Richard Henry Lee* (New York, 1911), II, 37-38. Cited hereafter as Ballagh, *Letters of Lee*. Henry Clinton to Lord George Germain, May 11, 1779, Clinton Papers.

[91] PCC, Roll 72, Item 59, I-II, 57.

[92] George Washington to Henry Clinton, March 14, 1779, Syrett and Cooke, *Papers of Hamilton*, II, 20.

[93] Henry Clinton to George Washington, March 31, 1779, BHQP, Reel 6, Document 1869.

[94] Colonel West Hyde and Captain John André to Henry Clinton, April 17, 1779, Clinton Papers.

[95] Colonel West Hyde and Captain John André to Henry Clinton, April 14, 1779, BHQP, Reel 6, Document 1917. Henry Clinton to Lord George Germain, May 11, 1779, Clinton Papers.

[96] George Washington to President of Congress, January 1, 1780, Fitzpatrick, *Writings of Washington*, XVII, 352-54.

[97] President of Congress to George Washington, January 27, 1780, Burnett, *Letters*, V, 17. JCC, XVI, 93-94.

[98] George Washington to Baron von Knyphausen, February 29, 1780, Fitzpatrick, *Writings of Washington,* XVII, 61.

[99] Baron von Knyphausen to George Washington, March 4, 1780, BHQP, Reel 8, Document 2614. Major General Arthur St. Clair and Lieu-

tenant Colonels Edward Carrington and Alexander Hamilton to George Washington, March 26, 1780, Syrett and Cooke, *Papers of Hamilton*, II, 295-96.

[100] Minutes of Meeting at Amboy, New Jersey, March 10-14, 1780, PCC, Roll 184, Item 167, 43-59. Also see BHQP, Reel 8, Document 2638.

[101] General Arthur St. Clair and Lieutenant Colonels Edward Carrington and Alexander Hamilton to George Washington, March 26, 1780, PCC, Roll 184, Item 167, 81-87. George Washington to President of Congress, March 31, 1780, Fitzpatrick, *Writings of Washington*, XVIII, 188.

[102] Joshua Loring to Abraham Skinner, June 21, 1780, Clinton Papers. Abraham Skinner to Joshua Loring, September 21, 1780, and Joshua Loring to Abraham Skinner, September 22, 1780, PCC, Roll 184, Item 167, 65-66, 69-73. Henry Clinton to George Washington, November 4, 1780, and November 29, 1780, BHQP, Reel 9, Documents 3133, 3165. George Washington to Henry Clinton, November 20, 1780, Fitzpatrick, *Writings of Washington*, XX, 375-76. JCC, XVIII, 1028, 1204.

[103] George Washington to President of Congress, November 7, 1780, Fitzpatrick, *Writings of Washington*, XX, 314-15.

[104] PCC, Roll 72, Item 59, I-II, 61.

[105] John Mathews to Nathanael Greene, April 30, 1781, Burnett, *Letters*, VI, 72. David Olyphant to Nathanael Greene, June 9, 1781, Greene Papers. George Washington to Abraham Skinner, June 14, 1781, Fitzpatrick, *Writings of Washington*, XXI, 214. George Washington to General Greene, October 31, 1781, *ibid.*, XXIII, 311.

[106] Benjamin Franklin to David Hartley, May 25, 1778, Smyth, *Writings of Franklin*, VII, 155-56. Alexander, "Forton Prison," 379.

[107] *Ibid.*

[108] Arthur Lee to Comte de Vergennes, June 14, 1778, Stevens, *Facsimiles*, VIII, Document 834, 4. Prelinger, "Benjamin Franklin," 273.

[109] L. H. Butterfield, ed., *Diary and Autobiography of John Adams* (Cambridge, Massachusetts, 1961), IV, 138-39. Cited hereafter as Butterfield, *Diary*.

[110] *Ibid.*

[111] Comte de Vergennes to Dr. Franklin, September 9, 1778, Stevens, *Facsimiles*, XXIII, Document 1956.

[112] Livesey, *Prisoners of 1776*, 231-32. Benjamin Franklin to John Adams, April 21, 1779, Smyth, *Writings of Franklin*, VII, 287-88.

[113] Cutter, "Yankee Privateersman," 285-86.

[114] Benjamin Franklin to John Jay, October 4, 1779, Smyth, *Writings of Franklin*, VII, 387.

[115] President of Congress to George Washington, December 5, 1781,

Burnett, *Letters*, VI, 273. George Washington to Abraham Skinner, December 12, 1781, Fitzpatrick, *Writings of Washington*, XXIII, 372.

[116] Proposed Rate of Exchange, April, 1779, PCC, Roll 35, Item 28, 16-17.

[117] Proposed Tariff by the Commissioner at Amboy, March, 1780, Mackenzie Papers.

[118] Joshua Loring to Abraham Skinner, February 12, 1782, BHQP, Reel 12, Document 4138.

[119] Joshua Loring to Abraham Skinner, January 20, 1782, *ibid.*, Document 4060. PCC, Roll 35, Item 128, 57. Henry Clinton to George Washington, February 11, 1782, BHQP, Reel 12, Document 4135.

[120] Benjamin Franklin to R. R. Livingston, March 30, 1782, Wharton, *Revolutionary Diplomatic Correspondence*, V, 277. Benjamin Franklin to John Jay, April 24, 1782, Johnston, *Correspondence of Jay*, II, 194. Anderson, "Treatment of American Prisoners," 67.

[121] James Madison to Edmund Pendleton, July 16, 1782, Burnett, *Letters*, VI, 385.

[122] Schedule of Proceedings at Tappan, BHQP, Reel 15, Document 5688.

[123] Michael Humble to Guy Carleton, August 19, 1782, *ibid.*, Document 5342.

[124] Thomas Carbill to Guy Carleton, August 25, 1782, *ibid.*, Document 5449.

[125] W. Brown to Guy Carleton, August 20, 1782, *ibid.*, Document 5350.

[126] George Harrison to Guy Carleton, August 20, 1782, *ibid.*, Document 5355.

[127] George Washington to William Stephen Smith, January 22, 1783, Fitzpatrick, *Writings of Washington*, XXVI, 59.

[128] George Washington to William Stephen Smith, March 3, 1783, *ibid.*, 177-78.

[129] Minutes of Conference between General George Washington and Sir Guy Carleton, Tappan, New York, May 6, 1783, *ibid.*, 402-6. Maryland Delegates to Governor of Maryland, May 6, 1783, Burnett, *Letters*, VII, 160.

[130] George Washington to the Secretary at War, July 1, 1783, Fitzpatrick, *Writings of Washington*, XXVII, 41.

[131] Benjamin Franklin to Robert R. Livingston, July 22, 1783, Smyth, *Writings of Franklin*, IX, 72.

Conclusion

Few attempts to assess British prisoner of war policy in detail appeared prior to the Second World War. Until the 1950's most of the accounts of Americans held prisoners of war were largely the letters, diaries, and memoirs of the men who were unfortunate enough to have been captives during the American Revolution, or the public papers of the men who participated in deciding the fate of the prisoners of war. In fact, there is an astonishing amount of such primary material, which was edited and published in the nineteeth and early twentieth centuries, available to the researcher. Such eyewitness information is vital to an understanding of the regimen endured by the captives, but, all too often, the claims of such documents were accepted with little critical analysis. Neither the authors nor the editors of these narratives were inclined to go beyond simply identifying people, places, and events.

Nearly all the literature regarding the plight of American captives produced by veterans of the American Revolution reflects a strong bias against Great Britain. Such a bias is not too surprising. It would be a little unreasonable to expect a former captive to produce a dispassionate account of his captivity and the conditions he had to overcome to survive. As a consequence, first person accounts are usually emphatic condemnations of Great Britain's prisoner of war program, and they frequently hint or assert that the hardships encountered by the captives were the result of a premeditated and vindictive policy of punishment. A few of the men who recorded their experiences while captives chose to refine their views slightly and occasionally offered the viewpoint that the mistreatment of prisoners of war was, in part, a ploy used by the British Army and Navy to discourage support for the Revolutionary cause and to coerce men into enlisting in the royal military forces. Rarely, however, does one find any effort to provide a detached evaluation of the circumstances surrounding the debacle attending the care of prisoners. Normally these accounts assume the worst possible motives on the part of the British when explaining the origin of the policies employed to control and care for captives. Former American prisoners of war were prone to speak poorly of their captors, and their readers were equally prone to accept the judgments of the men who inhabited the prisons.

An issue such as the treatment of prisoners requires the passage of a good deal of time before a balanced judgment can emerge. The narratives of the suffering of the prisoners were sometimes exaggerated, but the men did hunger, they were neglected, and they often experienced excruciating hardship. No one can honestly minimize or belittle the sacrifices of the American captives. That would be grossly unfair and inaccurate. What should be done, however, is to remember that the men who wrote of their time in prison were not too well qualified to pinpoint the reasons and rationale behind Great Britain's policies concerning prisoners. The British were not guilty of excessive disregard of the welfare of prisoners, and the conduct of the royal military authorities did not border on criminal action. The traditional view of the British action toward prisoners as being vicious is not just or fair.

The available evidence clearly indicates that the British Army and Navy were not guilty of a conscious policy of concerted cruelty in their conduct while caring for Americans languishing in their prisons. While the royal authorities can be exonerated of charges accusing them of officially harassing captives, they are vulnerable to sharp criticism relative to the shortcomings of the results of the actual policy which finally emerged concerning the welfare of the captives under their care. It should also be noted in passing that most of the deficiencies of the British program to provide adequate care for American prisoners of war can be detected among the policies established by American authorities to tend to the needs of British captives detained in prisons supervised by the rebellious state of national governments. Both warring camps compiled pitiful records in sustaining captives. Nevertheless, the British deserved censure in several categories regarding their treatment of captives. What must be remembered, however, is that the lack of effective protection of captives was not unique during the American Revolution. Both factions performed poorly in establishing an acceptable environment for their prisoners. The mutual failure of the combatants to see that justice was done to captured personnel does not justify the results of the British program, but it cannot be overlooked.

Most of the privations endured by Americans in British prisons arose from several areas of vital needs. One of the most frequent complaints listed by American captives was inadequate food. The basic policy of the British Army and Navy was to allocate a food allotment to captives which was equal to two-thirds the daily ration issued to British military personnel. The regulation food allotment for a British soldier or sailor was none too generous, and, consequently, it proved to be inadequate for captives. Food was not only doled out to captives in insufficient quantity, it was also a monotonous fare which prompted bitter protest. Additonally, there is ample evidence to assert that the quality of the food was doubtful. Most American captives were required to cope with rations which were not abundant, varied, or nutritious. Much of the shortage of food was based on the aforementioned assumption, mistaken as it was, that prisoners needed less food than men on active duty. So, on the matter of meager food rations, the logic is apparent even though the consequences were not pleasant to the captives.

The unvarying composition of the rations issued to the captives is another matter upon which the British can be partially excused. Eighteenth century technology and its limitations played a major role in the failure of the royal military forces to supply the men with a balanced and nutritious diet. Problems revolving about the acquisition, storing, shipping, preservation, and distribution of rations were virtually impossible to overcome. Considering the enormous task of feeding hundreds of men daily, the British had to provide the men with such items as salt meat, dried vegetables, flour, and other foodstuffs which were unlikely to spoil rapidly. It was a foregone conclusion among captors and captives that salt meat was not as palatable as fresh beef, but the British really could do little to alter the matter. Fresh vegetables and fruit would have improved the prisoners' diet, but how could such quantities as the men needed be supplied to them before they were ruined or rotten? Consequently, the lessened quality of the rations, and the monotonous regularity with which they appeared in the prison messes, can be explained more as a matter of logistics than from a desire to persecute captives.

The Continental Congress became deeply concerned about the increasing volume of complaints arising from the American captives regarding the limited rations and tried to do something to offer them some relief. Congress inaugurated a plan, with the consent of the British military authorities, to supplement the rations of the captives by sending food and money to the men, but it soon discovered it could do little to alter noticeably their daily rations except to provide larger amounts of the same sort of food already available to the prisoners. About the only real improvement Congress was able to foster was to send live cattle to the prison sites to be slaughtered to provision the men with fresh meat. Unfortunately for the men in the prisons, such shipments of cattle proved to be sporadic, and lasting change in the captives' way of life was not accomplished. Congress tried to help the men, but it failed. American prisoners of war sometimes received bigger portions of food, but, basically, the American government's intention of augmenting their diet fell far short of the needs of the men. So, in all fairness, it is not realistic to condemn the British for the food supplied the prisoners, since even the concerned Congress could do little to aid the men.

While the royal military forces honestly labored to supply the prisoners with what were, in their opinion, adequate food allotments, there were other deficiencies in the program designed to care for the captives which were less excusable. Allocations of clothing and bedding to the captives were uncommon. The British never adopted a standard policy governing this matter, and the men suffered as a result. Replacements of clothing and bedding, as infrequent as they were, usually came at the change of seasons, especially with the coming of winter. When the issues of apparel were made it did not mean that all the captives were included, and it did not mean that the prisoners got a complete supply of clothing and bedding. The shortcomings of the British care of prisoners in this area are not easy to explain. It involves a matter of attitude toward the prisoners rather than a problem of resources or logistics.

The basic cause for the paucity of replacement clothing for the captives was neglect on the part of the British. Neglect of the needs of the soldier or sailor, free or captive, seems to be one of the hallmarks of the war. On both sides, the men were often without many of the fundamental items a man might desire to have. How many times were men of the Continental Army thrown on their own ingenuity to clothe themselves? How many times were they awaiting back pay? The British soldier and sailor were better cared for in a material sense, but they were treated with a detachment by their own officers which bordered on an absence of concern over their actual welfare as human beings. When this attitude was translated into one regarding prisoners of war, the results were most unpleasant for the captives. The British high command rarely bothered itself to contemplate the plight of the captives, who often desperately required new clothing. As was the case with the food the American captives received, the assumption, on the part of the British Army, was that they were going to have to make do with what they had. The Congress tried to ship extra clothing to the men in the British prisons, but it accomplished little in relieving their distress. On this matter, the lack of good clothing, the British military authorities were open to censure.

On the matter of shelter, the British are again liable to criticism. Prisons developed to contain the captives varied enormously in quality, but they were usually bad. Understandably enough, barracks for the captives in the early phase of the war were whatever makeshift the army and navy could employ. To criticize the British for hardships endured by prisoners on or near the field of battle is unreasonable, but when the men were transferred to permanent prisons then the army and navy became more vulnerable to stringent criticism. In most cases, the prisons were buildings converted to detention centers and obviously lacked many of the characteristics of suitable prisons. Even that should not be too surprising in the early part of the war. Little fault can be assigned to the British as they struggled to establish a prison system under the pressure of the flood of captives taken by their highly successful campaigns early in the Revolution. As the war dragged on, however, the problem was compounded by the fact that the military authorities did nothing to improve substantially the prisons in which the American personnel were detained. At that juncture, the British authorities deserve censure.

The sugar house prisons in New York City are a good example. Quite obviously, the sugar houses were not designed to serve as prisons, yet they were so employed. And throughout the years they were used as prisons to detain captives, nothing was done to alter them except to render them barely capable of serving as prisons. Again and again, this pattern repeated itself during the war. On the heels of a victory, the army and navy pressed various types of buildings and vessels into use as prisons, altered them slightly to increase their security potential, and then never went beyond providing the barest essentials in seeing to prisoner welfare. As a result, the prisons were grim, dull, unhealthy, and unsanitary compounds. Much of the failure to provide clean, well-ordered prisons reflected the attitude of the eighteenth century rather than a desire to seek revenge upon helpless men, but the lack of effort to protect the captives from nearly intolerable circumstances was so apparent that the whole prison system can only be described as tragic.

The failure to create a program which would develop adequate shelter for the captives had several adverse effects on the men, but the most obvious and persistent problem was overcrowding the prisons. All manner of difficulties arose in the tightly packed compounds. The most obvious consequence of the teeming prisons was that the overcrowded conditions helped to induce poor health among the inmates. The packed prisons were especially burdensome among naval captives in the prison ships. Everything from common ailments to serious diseases spread easily among the prisoners. In addition to the physical problems, the overcrowded conditions of the prisons also created severe psychological and emotional stress for the men. The emotional strain was less apparent, but it was real. Examples of captives going berserk were frequent enough that many of the men who endured the prisons mention such incidents in their writings. Then, of course, there were the emotional scars left on the captives after they were released from captivity; these are not recorded, but they must be considered when one reflects upon the total effect of the prisons upon the inmates.

Medical care for the prisoners of war, on both sides, was minimal at best. Physicians who attempted to tend to the needs of the captives were limited by the fact that there were too few of them to see to the health and well-being of the prisoners, and they were restricted by the lack of knowledge or experience of how to cope with such awesome problems produced by numbers of men in small and unclean prisons. Probably the greatest criticism to be made against the British medical and military authorities, which can be leveled against the American program of prisoner care as well, is the failure to pursue any program of preventive medicine to forestall illnesses bred by the filth of the prisons. On occasion one can find records of prisons being scrubbed with vinegar, and of the captives being allowed to enjoy fresh air and sunshine, but this sort of circumstance was the exception rather than the rule. The medical personnel who attended the captives were aware of the salutory benefits of such action, but they did not see fit to enforce such rules or procedures for their patients. A little more concern about such matters as enforced personal hygiene programs would have been of enormous benefit to the prisoners of war in all camps. The captives were forced by circumstances and environment into slovenly habits, and the captors did nothing to clean or air the prisons; as a result, the filth helped to breed or perpetuate sickness among the men. The capacity to neglect or to overlook the basic needs of helpless individuals is a hideous but universal trait of all nationalities of mankind.

Another factor which partially explains the dismal conditions endured by the captives early in the war was the expectation, on the part of Great Britain, of a short-lived struggle. At the outset of hostilities, the war appeared to be the worst kind of mismatch, with all the critical resources to wage effective war deposited in the hands of the royal military authorities. General William Howe, the British Commander in Chief from 1776 to early 1778, was aware of his advantages, and, because of the confidence his assets prompted, he never seemed willing to consider a long term plan to care for large numbers of captives. Howe did not anticipate a protracted war, and he patiently awaited the collapse of colonial resistance in the wake of his successful campaigns. Consequently, he did little to see to the needs of prisoners except to proffer minimum support based upon the assumption that the war would soon end. Royal military figures all viewed issues regarding prison compounds, clothing and food allotments, medical care, and exchanges of captives as transient ones, since the war was supposed to end quickly. Decisions regarding prisoner welfare were always, in the early years of the war, predicated on the belief that any expediency would suffice, since the problem would soon cease to exist.

It is well to remember that the years of 1776 and 1777, until the peak of 1780, were the period when American captives in British prisons were most numerous. The combination of Howe's optimistic and short-sighted policy plus the overcrowded prisons produced unfortunate results for men incarcerated in them. As the prisons bulged with captives, General Howe continued to operate his prisons upon the assumption that the war would soon be concluded, and a general exchange of prisoners would be forthcoming. So, for nearly two years, the official British response to the pressing needs of the captives was to act on the hope that the war was about to end and to devote as few resources to caring for the captives as was humanely possible. The defeat of General John Burgoyne's army in 1777 revealed the futility of Howe's expectations.

In 1777, as any student of the American Revolution knows, General Burgoyne led an expedition of more than seven thousand men out of Canada and invaded New York. After several weeks of campaigning, General Burgoyne's army was finally trapped at Saratoga, New York, and he was forced to surrender his entire command to the victorious troops under the direction of General Horatio Gates. Several changes in the prisoner of war controversy were fostered by Burgoyne's ill-fated campaign of 1777. For the first time the American authorities had a large number of British captives to use in bargaining with the British Army in an effort to improve the conditions encountered by Americans in enemy prisons. Significantly, diaries of prisoners often mention an increase of food allotments and other favorable alterations in daily prison life shortly after the capture of Burgoyne's forces. Obviously, Howe's concern for the welfare of prisoners became a less one-sided affair when he had to consider the fate of so many of his own men. Howe fully understood that the treatment his men received would, in part, be conditioned by his response to the needs of American personnel under his supervision. Additionally, the British Army, which needed manpower desperately, manifested a renewed and sincere interest in equitable prisoner exchanges after General Burgoyne's army was marched off to American prison camps. And best of all for American prisoners of war, the British Army reluctantly admitted that the war was going to last longer than previously expected. Therefore, the royal military leaders expressed a tentative desire to engage in discussions which might lead to mutual agreements regarding reforms to improve the lives of all captives. Such a realization caused the British to begin to negotiate more openly and fully with the rebel forces and to reform their thinking in regard to the needs of American captives. Ultimately, the improvements in the daily lives of American prisoners were not massive in nature, but the dwindling numbers of men in the prison centers found that their routine was a bit more acceptable in the late 1770's.

In the beginning, General Howe was inclined to overlook the hardships occasioned by his prisons upon the colonials in the belief that they would soon be released anyway. He seemed to think that a few sacrifices, on the part of the prisoners, were to be expected even under the best of circumstances. Such an attitude on General Howe's part prompted most of the privations experienced by the captives. Howe should not, however, be too heavily censured for his actions. His decision not to work toward a long-range, permanent prisoner care policy was based on the best information and common sense available in 1776. No one could predict a war of seven years' length considering the colonials' lack of unity and resources to wage war at that point. Consequently, Howe tried to avoid a costly and elaborate program to look after captives in what he was certain was a short-term problem at the most. Logic, it appeared, supported his position, but he was wrong. The first two years of the war were a time of error and confusion on both sides, which led to discomfort for all captives. British captives residing in American prisons did not fare much better than did the personnel under the jurisdiction of British military authorities in this early phase of the war. Both warring camps at the outset failed to grasp the significance of a lengthy conflict for the mounting numbers of prisoners which the war finally forced them to recognize by 1778. Few men outside the prisons fully comprehended the magnitude of the problems of caring for men under detention or satisfying their needs and desires.

Another feature, already mentioned but worth repeating, which handicapped any rapid agreement on policy governing the treatment of captives was the legal question of the status of American prisoners of war. The fundamental issue was whether, in fact, to deal with the Americans as rebels or as prisoners of war. General Howe and his successors in the post of supreme commander of British forces in America had a delicate problem to ponder when dealing with the captured colonials. Americans, from the viewpoint of Great Britain, were in revolt against their legitimate government and therefore could not claim the traditional rights of prisoners of war. The British government vacillated on the issue of whether to treat the men as nothing more than rebels with the stringent consequences that meant, but, in the meantime, dealt with the captured American personnel rather gently.

Instead of trying the captives for treason, which would have been quite legal, and punishing them for the crime of insurrection, which would have been unwise, the British government chose to deal with the captives as if they were prisoners of war without officially declaring them such until the last year of the conflict. In a few isolated instances the treatment accorded American captives was not equal to that traditionally provided to captured enemy personnel in wartime, but, for all practical purposes, Great Britain acted with admirable restraint and calm throughout the whole crisis and did not surrender to the temptation of meting out harsh punishment to the rebels. The legal question about the status of American captives did, however, pose a thorny problem for the British military leaders in the field. Any attempt to negotiate agreements governing any aspect of prisoner care or exchange had to be approached with great caution and in very precise language. Any joint agreement between American and British representatives to safeguard prisoners which might be couched in the wrong language might possibly be interpreted as a tacit recognition of American independence and might further encourage Great Britain's enemies to bolder action in behalf of the colonies. Fearful of opening new political and diplomatic quarrels elsewhere in the world, the British Army proved a reluctant party to discuss even the most inane issues with American leaders early in the war.

Consequently, when the British did negotiate, they moved with a wariness which seldom produced concrete results. Americans often jumped to the conclusion that Howe and his successors were insincere about seeking improvements in the prison conditions rather than understanding the difficult position of the British Army as a negotiating force. The royal military leaders were remote from London, and their instructions were not always reflective of the current mood of their political leaders. Howe's major problem, which was shared by the men who succeeded him in command in America, was the constant dread of entering into an arrangement with the American Army to help captives, and, in so doing, opening the door to an American claim of his having recognized their government. When meetings were convened to discuss ways and means to protect or assist captives there was one major point upon which the conferences often foundered. British negotiating teams could enter into agreements with their American counterparts only if the American representatives would accept the arrangements secured by the word and honor of the British supreme commander. The British officers could not pledge the word of their government to support officially whatever issue they were trying to resolve, as such a move could be interpreted as a *de facto* recognition of American independence. American commissioners, on the other hand, usually insisted that the word of the British government be pledged to uphold whatever arrangements the conference might establish concerning the issues revolving about prisoner welfare.

The American position regarding exchange agreements was not without its merits. Certainly there was some political advantage in dealing directly with the British government, but, more importantly, an agreement with the government in London would be lasting in character. The military commanders in America were not permanent figures. If an agreement was based upon the honor of a commander and he was removed from his position then the arrangement could be suspended unless his successor chose to accept it. The perils of concluding an agreement with an individual commander were obvious. As a result of all the maneuvering for political position between the adversaries, reforms for prisoner welfare were slow to appear. All too often the prisoners were not much more than pawns in a massive struggle complicated by political and diplomatic issues. It is apparent that the belligerents occasionally used the prisoner of war issue shamelessly while seeking other goals. Cynical use of prisoners of war by warring nations to secure political concession is not unique, but the results for those forced to endure incarceration while the game is being played often are tragic. Both sides, it should be noted, believed that their claims were justified and fought for recognition of their principles, but many men endured difficult times while their governments seemed to quarrel endlessly.

Prisoners of war did suffer during the American Revolution. There is no other conclusion which can be reached regarding captives on both sides. Men were beaten, deprived of food by corrupt officials, denied bedding and clothing, and harassed in other ways, but, fortunately, such incidents of outright cruelty were not the most common of events. Actually, most of the suffering of the men came from more subtle torment usually brought on by neglect of their needs or by inattention to them. Neither the British nor American authorities sought to induce the suffering of the men in their prisons, yet the men did want for basic services. The shortcomings of both sides in providing for the captives were evident, but the motivations behind the failure to provide for the captives in an acceptable fashion were not evil or vindictive in nature. Neither party entered into a program of deliberately tormenting prisoners. Rather, the failure to support prisoners adequately stemmed from the complicated issues surrounding what was then a unique war. The limitations of the eighteenth century also contributed to the lack of care of the captives, and it can be asserted that the eighteenth century military mind was not overly concerned with welfare of the unfortunate men who became prisoners of war. Judged by modern standards, Great Britain could be charged with gross neglect of the captives in the military prisons. But, on the other hand, recent wars in this century have established records of barbarity toward prisoners of war which are truly terrifying. The British did not use torture, ideological assault, or other extreme forms of punishment upon helpless men. The British response to the issue of American prisoners of war was not always handled well, and in many instances it lacked direction and effective control, but British policy could not be typified as cruel.

Bibliography

Manuscripts

British Headquarters Papers, New York Public Library photostats, New York, New York.

Boudinot Ledger, 1760-1814, New York Public Library, New York, New York.

Boudinot Papers, The Historical Society of Pennsylvania, Philadelphia, Pennsylvania.

Sir Henry Clinton Papers, William L. Clements Library, Ann Arbor, Michigan.

General Thomas Gage Papers, William L. Clements Library, Ann Arbor, Michigan.

Lord George Germain Papers, William L. Clements Library, Ann Arbor, Michigan.

Nathanael Greene Papers, Library of Congress, Washington, D. C.

Nathanael Greene Papers, William L. Clements Library, Ann Arbor, Michigan.

William Livingston, Seven Letters between Governor Livingston of New Jersey and Sir Guy Carleton, May 7, 1782, to July 25, 1782, concerning treatment of prisoners of war. New York Public Library, New York, New York.

Frederick Mackenzie Papers, William L. Clements Library, Ann Arbor, Michigan.

Lord North Papers, William L. Clements Library, Ann Arbor, Michigan.

Papers of the Continental Congress, National Archives Microfilm Publication, Washington, D. C.

Reminiscences of the Early Life of John Pintard, the New-York Historical Society, New York, New York.

Lewis Pintard Papers, The New-York Historical Society, New York, New York.

"Some Account of the capture of the ship Aurora," Phillip Freneau Collection, Rutgers University Library, New Brunswick, New Jersey.

Washington Papers, Library of Congress, Washington, D. C.

Printed Sources and Contemporary Accounts

Abbatt, William, ed., *Memoirs of Major-General William Heath*. New York, 1968.

Adams, Charles Francis, ed., *The Works of John Adams*. 10 vols. Boston, 1850-1856.

Allaire, Anthony, *Diary of Lieutenant Anthony Allaire*. New York, 1968.

Allen, Ethan, *Allen's Captivity, being a Narrative of Colonel Ethan Allen*. Boston, 1845.

Andros, Thomas, *The Old Jersey Captive: or, A Narrative of the Captivity of Thomas Andros (now Pastor of the Church in Berkley) on board the old Jersey Prison ship at New York, 1781*. Boston, 1833.

Annual Register.

Ballagh, James Curtis, ed., *The Letters of Richard Henry Lee*. 2 vols. New York, 1911.

Banks, James Lennox, ed., *David Sproat and Naval Prisoners in the War of the Revolution*. New York, 1909.

Barclay, Sidney, ed., *Personal Recollections of the American Revolution, A Private Journal Prepared from Authentic Domestic Records by Lydia Minturn Post*. Port Washington, New York, 1970.

Barnes, John S., ed., *Fanning's Narrative, Being the Memoirs of Nathaniel Fanning An Officer of the Revolutionary Navy, 1778-1783*. New York,

1968.

Boudinot, Elias, *Journal or Historical Recollections of American Events During the Revolutionary War.* Philadelphia, 1894.

Boudinot, J. J., ed., *The Life, Public Services, Addresses and Letters of Elias Boudinot, L.L.D., President of the Continental Congress.* 2 vols. Cambridge, Massachusetts, 1896.

Bowden, William Hammond, ed., "Diary of William Widger of Marblehead, Kept at Mill Prison, England, 1781," *The Essex Institute Historical Collections*, LXXIII (1937), LXXIV (1938), 311-47, 22-48.

Boyd, Julian P., ed., *The Papers of Thomas Jefferson*, 18 vols. Princeton, 1950-1972.

Browne, William Hand, (et. al.), ed., *Archives of Maryland.* 65 vols. Baltimore, 1883-1952.

Burnett, E. C., ed., *Letters of Members of the Continental Congress.* 8 vols. Washington, D. C., 1921-1938.

Bushell, Charles I., ed., *A Narrative of the Life and Adventures of Levi Hanford, A Soldier of the Revolution.* New York, 1863.

_____, ed., *The Adventures of Christopher Hawkins.* New York, 1864.

_____, ed., *The Narrative of John Blatchford*, New York, 1865.

Butterfield, L. H., ed., *Diary and Autobiography of John Adams.* 4 vols. Cambridge, Massachusetts, 1961.

_____, ed., *Letters of Benjamin Rush.* 2 vols. Princeton, 1951.

Cornelius, Elias, *Journal of Dr. Elias Cornelius, A Revolutionary Surgeon and Biographical Sketch.* Washington, D. C., 1903.

Clinton, Henry, *The American Rebellion, Sir Henry Clinton's Narrative of His Campaigns, 1775-1782, with an appendix of Original Documents.* Ed. William B. Willcox. New Haven, 1954.

Collins, Varnum Lansing, ed., *A Brief Narrative of the Ravages of the British and Hessians at Princeton in 1776-1777.* New York, 1968.

Cutter, William R., ed., "A Yankee Privateersman in Prison in England, 1777-1779," *The New England Historical and Genealogical Register*, XXX (1876), 174-77, 343-52.

Dandridge, Danske, ed., *American Prisoners of the Revolution*. Baltimore, 1967.

Fitch, Jabez, *The New York Diary of Lieutenant Jabez Fitch*. Ed. W. H. W. Sabine, New York, 1954.

Fitzpatrick, John C., ed., *The Writings of George Washington*. 39 vols. Washington, D. C., 1931-1944.

Force, Peter, ed., *American Archives*. 5th Series, 3 vols. Washington, D. C., 1837-1853.

Ford, Worthington Chauncey, ed., *Letters of William Lee, 1776-1783*. 3 vols. New York, 1891.

_____, (et. al), eds., *The Journals of the Continental Congress, 1774-1789*. Washington, D. C., 1904-1937.

_____, ed., "British and American Prisoners of War, 1778," *The Pennsylvania Magazine of History and Biography*, XVII (1893), 159-74, 316-24.

Fortescue, John, ed., *The Correspondence of King George the Third with Lord North from 1768 to December 1783*. 6 vols. London, 1927-1928.

Gentlemen's Magazine and Historical Chronicle.

George, Lord Rodney, *Letter-Books and Order-Book of George, Lord Rodney Admiral of the White Squadron, 1780-1782*. 2 vols. New York, 1932.

Gibbes, R. W., ed., *Documentary History of the American Revolution Consisting of Letters and Papers Relating to the Contest for Liberty Chiefly in South Carolina, In 1781 and 1782*. Columbia, South Carolina, 1853.

Greene, Albert G., ed., *Recollections of the Jersey Prisonship; Taken and Prepared for Publication from the Original Manuscripts of the Late Captain Thomas Dring of Providence, R. I.* Providence, Rhode Island, 1829.

Hall, Charles S., ed., *Life and Letters of Samuel Holden Parsons*. Binghamton, New York, 1965.

Heitman, F. B., ed., *Historical Register of Officers of the Continental Army During the Revolution*. Washington, D. C., 1892.

Historical Manuscripts Commission, *Report on American Manuscripts in the Royal Institution of Great Britain*. 4 vols. London, 1904-1909.

_____, *Report on Manuscripts in Various Collections*. 8

vols. London, 1904-1909.

Headly, Charles J. and L. W. Larabee, eds., *Public Records of the State of Connecticut.* 8 vols. Hartford, 1894-1951.

Hutchinson, William T. and William M. E. Rachal, eds., *The Papers of James Madison.* 8 vols. Chicago, 1962-1973.

Johnston, Henry P., ed., *The Correspondence and Public Papers of John Jay.* 4 vols. New York, 1890-1893.

Jones, Thomas, *History of New York During the Revolutionary War.* Ed. Floyd de Lancey. 2 vols. New York, 1879.

Jordan, Helen, ed., "Colonel Elias Boudinot in New York City, February, 1778," *The Pennsylvania Magazine of History and Biography*, XXIV (1900), 453-66.

"Journal of Samuel Cutler," *The New England Historical and Genealogical Register*, XXXII (1878), 42-44, 184-88, 305-8, 395-98.

Lafayette, George Washington, ed., *Memoirs, Correspondence and Manuscripts of General Lafayette*, London, 1837.

Laurens, Henry, "Narrative of his Capture, of his Confinement in the Tower of London etc. 1780, 1781, 1782," *South Carolina Historical Society Collections.* I (1857), 18-83.

Lee, Henry, *Memoirs of the War in the Southern Department of the United States.* Ed. Robert E. Lee. New York, 1869.

"Letters of Joseph Clay, Merchant of Savannah, 1776-1793," *Collections of the Georgia Historical Society.* Vol. 7, Savannah, 1913.

Littell, John S., ed., *Memoirs of His own Time with Reminiscences of the Men and Events of the Revolution by Alexander Graydon.* Philadelphia, 1846.

Livesey, Rev. R., ed., *The Prisoners of 1776; A Relic of the Revolution.* Boston, 1854.

Mays, David J., ed., *The Letters and Papers of Edmund Pendleton, 1721-1803.* 2 vols. Cambridge, Massachusetts, 1952.

McIlwaine, H. R., ed., *Official Letters of the Governors of the State of Virginia.* 3 vols. Richmond, 1926-1929.

Moody, James, *Lieutenant James Moody's Narrative of His Exertions and Sufferings in the Cause of Government Since the Year 1776; Authenticated By Proper Certificates.* New York, 1968.

Moore, Frank, ed., *Diary of the American Revolution.* 2 vols. New York,

1860.

Onderdonck, Henry, *Revolutionary Incidents of Suffolk and King's Counties: with an Account of the Battle of Long Island and the British Prison-ships at New York.* New York, 1849.

Peckham, Howard H., ed., *Memoirs of the Life of John Adlum in the Revolutionary War.* Chicago, 1968.

Pettengill, R. W., ed., *Letters From America, 1776-1779: Being Letters of Brunswick, Hessian, and Waldeck Officers with the British Armies During the Revolution.* Port Washington, New York, 1964.

Potter, Israel Ralph, *Life and Adventures of Israel Ralph Potter.* New York, 1911.

Palmer, W. P., ed., *Calendar of Virginia State Papers and Other Manuscripts, 1652-1781.* 11 vols. New York, 1968.

"Papers of the First Council of Safety of the Revolutionary Party in South Carolina, June-November, 1775," *The South Carolina Historical and Genealogical Magazine,* II (1902), 1-26.

Ramsay, David, *Ramsay's History of South Carolina, From Its First Settlement In 1670 to the Year 1808.* Newberry, South Carolina, 1858.

Ross, Charles, ed., *Correspondence of Charles, First Marquis Cornwallis.* 3 vols. London, 1859.

Ryder, George Herbert, ed., *Letters to and from Caesar Rodney, 1756-1784.* Philadelphia, 1933.

Sterling, David L., ed., "American Prisoners of War in New York: A Report by Elias Boudinot," *The William and Mary Quarterly,* XIII (1956), 376-93.

Stevens, B. F., ed., *Facsimiles of Manuscripts in European Archives Relating to America 1773-1782.* 25 vols. London, 1889-1895.

Stiles, Henry R., ed., *Letters From the Prisons and Prison-Ships of the Revolution.* New York, 1865.

Stone, Hiram, ed., "The Experiences of a Prisoner in the American Revolution," *The Journal of American History,* II (1908), 527-29.

Smyth, Albert H., ed., *The Writings of Benjamin Franklin.* 10 vols. New York, 1905-1907.

Sparks, Jared, ed., *Correspondence of the American Revolution Being Letters of Eminent Men to George Washington.* 4 vols. Boston, 1853.

Syrett, Harold C. and Jacob E. Cooke, eds., *The Papers of Alexander*

Hamilton. 19 vols. New York, 1961-1973.

Tatum, Edward H., Jr., ed., *The Americán Journal of Ambrose Serle, Secretary to Lord Howe, 1776-1778.* San Marino, California, 1940.

Thatcher, James, *A Military Journal during the American Revolutionary War.* Boston, 1823.

The Royal Gazette, (South Carolina).

The Town and Country Magazine or Universal Repository of Knowledge, Instruction and Entertainment.

Tarleton, Banastre, *A History of the Campaigns of 1780 and 1781 in the Southern Provinces of North America.* New York, 1968.

Wharton, Francis, ed., *Revolutionary Diplomatic Correspondence.* 6 vols. Washington, D. C., 1889.

Secondary Works

Abell, Francis, *Prisoners of War in Britain, 1756-1815.* London, 1914.

Alexander, John K., "American Privateersmen In the Mill Prison During 1777-1782: An Evaluation," *The Essex Institute Historical Collections*, CII (1966), 318-40.

—————————, "Forton Prison During the American Revolution: A Case Study of The British Prisoner of War Policy and the American Prisoner Response to That Policy," *The Essex Institute Historical Collections*, CIII (1967), 365-89.

Allen, Gardner W., *A Naval History of the American Revolution.* 2 vols. Boston, 1913.

Amerman, Richard H., "Treatment of American Prisoners During the Revolution," *New Jersey Historical Society Proceedings*, LXXVIII (1960), 257-75.

Anderson, Olive, "The Treatment of Prisoners of War during the American War of Independence," *Bulletin of the Institute of Historical Research*, XXVIII (1955), 63-83.

Armbruster, Eugene L., *The Wallabout Prison Ships.* New York, 1920.

Bowman, Larry, "The Court-Martial of Captain Richard Lippincot," *New Jersey History*, LXXXIX (1971), 23-36.

Burnett, Edmund C., *The Continental Congress.* New York, 1941.

Coggins, Jack, *Ships and Seamen of the American Revolution.* Harrisburg, Pennsylvania, 1969.

Duyckinck, Evert A., ed., *Poems Relating to the American Revolution by Philip Freneau.* New York, 1865.

Fortescue, John W., *A History of the British Army.* 13 vols. London, 1899-1930.

Greene, George Washington, *The Life of Nathanael Greene.* 3 vols. New York, 1871.

Gruber, Ira G., *The Howe Brothers And The American Revolution.* New York, 1975.

Huguenin, Charles A., "Ethan Allen, Parolee on Long Island," *Vermont History*, XXV (1907), 103-25.

Jervey, Theodore D., "The Hayne Family," *The South Carolina Historical and Genealogical Magazine*, V (1904), 168-88.

Landrum, John B. O., *Colonial and Revolutionary History of Upper South Carolina.* Greenville, South Carolina, 1897.

Leary, Lewis, *That Rascal Freneau.* New Brunswick, New Jersey, 1941.

Lindsey, William R., "Treatment of American Prisoners of War During the Revolution," *The Emporia State Research Studies*, XXII (1973), 5-32.

Mayo, Katherine, *General Washington's Dilemma.* New York, 1938.

Metzger, Charles, S. J., *The Prisoner in the American Revolution.* Chicago, 1971.

Pintard, John, "The Old Jail," *The New York Mirror: A Weekly Devoted to Literature and the Fine Arts*, IX (1831), 1-2.

Prelinger, Catherine M., "Benjamin Franklin And The American Prisoners of War in England During The American Revolution," *The William and Mary Quarterly*, XXXII (1975), 261-94.

Rhett, Robert Goodwyn, *Charleston an Epic of Carolina.* Richmond, 1940.

Richards, Henry M. M., "The Pennsylvania-Germans in the British Military Prisons of the Revolutionary War," *The Pennsylvania-German Society Proceedings and Addresses*, XXXII (1924), 5-33.

Rowland, Kate M., *The Life of George Mason.* 2 vols. New York, 1892.

Sabine, Lorenzo, *Biographical Sketches of Loyalists of the American Revolution with an Historical Essay.* 2 vols. Port Washington, New

York, 1966.

Salley, A. S., Jr., "Capt. John Colcock and Some of His Descendants," *The South Carolina Historical and Genealogical Magazine*, III (1902), 216-41.

Shy, John, *Toward Lexington, The Role of the British Army in the Coming of the Revolution.* Princeton, 1965.

Snowden, Yates, ed., *History of South Carolina.* 5 vols. Chicago, 1920.

Stokes, L. N. P., *Iconography of Manhattan Island.* 6 vols. New York, 1895-1928.

Ward, Christopher, *The War of the Revolution.* Ed. John Richard Alden. 2 vols. New York, 1952.

Wertenbaker, Thomas Jefferson, *Father Knickerbocker Rebels: New York City During the Revolution.* New York, 1948.

West, Charles E., "Prison Ships in the American Revolution," *Journal of American History*, V (1911), 121-28.

Wilson, James Grant, *The Memorial History of the City of New York.* 4 vols. New York, 1892-1893.

INDEX